CASE STUDIES IN

CULTURAL ANTHROPOLOGY

GENERAL EDITORS
George and Louise Spindler
STANFORD UNIVERSITY

APPALACHIAN VALLEY

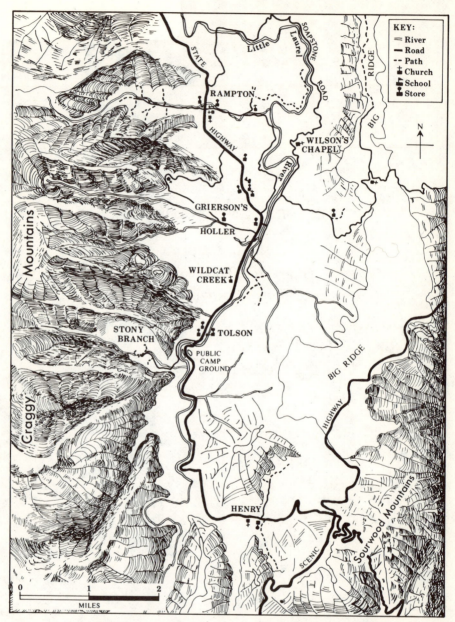

KEY:
≡ River
━ Road
-- Path
♦ Church
🏫 School
🏪 Store

Mountains

State

Highway

Little

Laurel

Soapstone

Road

Big

Ridge

N

RAMPTON

WILSON'S
CHAPEL

River

GRIERSON'S

HOLLER

WILDCAT
CREEK

STONY
BRANCH

TOLSON

PUBLIC
CAMP
GROUND

BIG RIDGE

Craggy

Highway

HENRY

Scenic

Sourwood Mountains

0   1   2
MILES

The Little Laurel Valley (map by Eugenia Robinson)

APPALACHIAN VALLEY

By

GEORGE L. HICKS

Brown University

HOLT, RINEHART AND WINSTON

NEW YORK   CHICAGO   SAN FRANCISCO   ATLANTA
DALLAS   MONTREAL   TORONTO   LONDON   SYDNEY

For my parents

Foreword

ABOUT THE SERIES

These case studies in cultural anthropology are designed to bring to students, in beginning and intermediate courses in the social sciences, insights into the richness and complexity of human life as it is lived in different ways and in different places. They are written by men and women who have lived in the societies they write about and who are professionally trained as observers and interpreters of human behavior. The authors are also teachers, and in writing their books they have kept the students who will read them foremost in their minds. It is our belief that when an understanding of ways of life very different from one's own is gained, abstractions and generalizations about social structure, cultural values, subsistence techniques, and the other universal categories of human social behavior become meaningful.

ABOUT THE AUTHOR

George L. Hicks is associate professor in the Department of Anthropology, Brown University. After receiving his master's degree in American history from the University of California, Berkeley, he shifted to anthropology by working for a year as archaeologist's assistant in the Research Laboratory of Anthropology, University of North Carolina, Chapel Hill, and then entering the graduate program in cultural anthropology at the University of Illinois, Urbana. He received his Ph.D. in anthropology from Illinois in 1969. As a predoctoral training fellow of the Social Science Research Council, and as a doctoral fellow of the Richard D. Irwin Foundation, he conducted fieldwork in 1965–1967 in the valley described in this book, among the local residents and the members of a cooperative community of ex-urbanites. This fieldwork, and his shorter periods of research on American Indian groups in the eastern United States, are only one part of a long-term research project into a number of aspects of American society and culture. At the present time, he is interested primarily in ethnicity in complex societies and in 1973–1974 he carried out fieldwork in the Azore Islands on Portuguese immigration to the United States and Canada. Like many of the people of Southern Appalachia, Mr. Hicks considers himself an American migrant, having been born and reared in the Deep South and later moving to the urban and industrial Northeast. And like the mountain migrants, he makes regular visits to his native territory.

ABOUT THE BOOK

By 1790 there were probably less than 100 white persons in the Little Laurel Valley. During the later westward migrations the Little Laurel became more rather than less isolated because there were easier routes around rather than through the valley. This isolation persisted until approximately World War II. With new highways traversing the area, accessibility to markets and market towns, commuting to work in nearby small industries, and particularly with the proliferation of TV sets the Little Laurel Valley can no longer be said to be isolated from the mainstream of American culture. Nevertheless it continues as a culturally distinct entity—a distinction that is displayed in local attitudes, speech, kinship relationships, and a strongly felt identity. This identity is not that presented in the images of L'il Abner, Mammy Yokum, or Snuffy Smith. It is an identity based upon a knowledge or an intuition of difference, but this difference is positive. There is also nostalgia for a past of greater cohesiveness, less disturbance from the outside, and greater trust.

The folk culture of the Appalachians is a significant part of the valued national imagery, irrespective of the comical and caricatured features of the hillbilly image. But whatever the imagery from the outside, the culture from the inside assumes different forms, shapes, and patterns of meaning. George Hicks develops this inside view with compassionate objectivity—the ideal stance of the anthropologist. He and his family were valued members of the community for more than a year and, as he writes, their personal persuasions were congruent with the community within which they lived and were accepted.

To the student of American culture *Appalachian Valley* is of special significance. Though tales of the preservation of "Elizabethan English" are indeed exaggerated, nevertheless, the relative isolation of the Little Laurel Valley and its culture means that it is both distinctive and continuous with an earlier colonial American culture. As one reads this case study, however, one is struck by the continuities with other areas of rural America. The strong emphasis upon egalitarianism, the resentment of any form of authoritarian "ordering around," the belief in personal independence and individualism, the sharp lines of demarkation between the world of women and the world of men, the suspicion of urban things and people, and the strong value placed upon rural life and the household within it, are all values found prominently in the culture of the Little Laurel Valley. If one goes further in the search for cultural similarities, it is not difficult to demonstrate that the small English rural community such as Hennage in East Anglia described by Clement Harris in this series exhibits many of these same cultural characteristics. This is not unexpected since the vast majority of surnames in the Little Laurel Valley are English, Scotch, and Irish. Hennage is, in some ways, more insulated from the outside world than the Little Laurel Valley. It is more turned upon itself and its own stability, and above all, to a social structure of estate or owners, gentry, and tenant farmers, that is lacking in the United States. However, the emphasis upon egalitarianism, resistance to authority, the ethic of noninterference, and a positive value for modest competence in many areas of activity as well as the separation of men's and women's worlds, even specific features of sexual relationships, appear to be very similar. If one moves out of the rural context to a contemporary segment of an urban community in the United States, as represented by the Portland longshoremen described by William Pilcher, one finds, again, many of these same general cultural features. The longshoremen reject the concept of social mobility as intrinsically worthless and agree wholeheartedly upon the principle of social egalitarianism. They place a high value on freedom from routine and rigid scheduling that sounds very much like an Appalachian attitude. There is the same sharp division of sex roles with women managing the domestic side, masculine conversations terminated when women appear on the scene, and masculine dominance in external or public affairs. There is also the same orientation towards multiple occupations and broad competence as in Appalachia. And men joke, boisterously, by innuendo, and with an ear to implications that escape the eye and ear of the outsider, just as in Appalachia and elsewhere in the broad Anglo-European based culture of North America.

Seen in this perspective the culture of the Little Laurel of Appalachia is not so much an exception as a rule. This local culture of long standing, embedded in a regional culture of distinction, is also representative of much that is old-line American. Americans of Anglo-American extraction may find something of their identity here that has been overshadowed and corroded by the material affluence, crassness, and immorality endemic in the American mainstream at present.

GEORGE AND LOUISE SPINDLER
General Editors

Stanford, California

Acknowledgments

The fieldwork on which this account is based was done, as is explained in Chapter 1, at various times from June 1965 to August 1967 and afterward. Financial support came from the Social Science Research Council (predoctoral training fellowship) and from a doctoral fellowship from the Richard D. Irwin Foundation. Both are gratefully acknowledged.

In return for the many helpful hours spent with me by patient informants and public officials, I have only anonymity to offer in return. All names of persons and places (except the names of states) have been changed to protect individuals. This has entailed, in some cases, the inclusion of quotations that are not attributed.

Some portions of Chapters 8 and 9 appeared in my article, "The War on Poverty: A Southern Appalachian Case," *Journal of the Steward Anthropological Society* (1972), 3:155–171. Kitchul Lee, a graduate student in anthropology at Brown University, spent several hours enlarging the photographs, a labor for which I am very appreciative.

For the eager cooperation and aid of my wife, Linné H. Hicks, and my daughter, Beth, there are no adequate means of expressing appreciation, and I will not try. Besides, they liked our life in the Little Laurel as much as I did.

G. L. H.

Contents

1 / Introduction: studying the Little Laurel

It was not the mountain people described in this book that originally attracted me to the Little Laurel Valley. I set out, in June 1965, to do a year of fieldwork in a cooperative community there. This small group of ex-urbanites, numbering sixty-seven, was to be the subject of my Ph.D. dissertation. But, in the first few months of work among them, I became very interested in their neighbors, the mountain people of the Little Laurel. Soon I found myself with two fieldwork projects going at the same time.

To gather information about the relations that existed between the cooperative community and local residents, it was necessary to spend time with people in both categories. Thus, after an initial three months in the community's guest cottage, I rented a house and moved with my wife and ten-year-old daughter to live in a local neighborhood.

Shortly after changing my residence, I accidentally overheard a rumor among local people that I had been labeled an "FBI man," a term of special scorn in the Little Laurel. Several months of patiently explaining my presence to various people, especially storekeepers, quieted the rumor that I was connected with the federal government. At other times, I was called a "psychiatrist," a "tourist," and a "schoolteacher." These appellations indicated that I was considered an outsider or, as elderly people said, a "furriner." Fully six months went by before my position as a student of local history and a curious observer of "the community people" (as the cooperative community is known) was satisfactorily established.

While casting me in the role of "FBI man" reflected the fear of some locals that their illegal activities in the national forest might be uncovered and punished, it seems to have been, for most, a means by which they could affirm their suspicions of the cooperative community and its residents. They have for many years considered "the community" to be a site of mysterious and unpatriotic activity. It therefore made a great deal of sense that the federal government would eventually send an investigator to find out what actually went on. The longer I stayed, however, the more willing were people to accept me as a person with whom they could indulge their pleasure in talking about themselves. My curiosity about "the community people" soon became just one aspect of my interest in local history and customs. Few people had any conception of what an anthropologist was, and I explained my study as an historical one. This seemed to satisfy everyone. My questions about "how things used to be," about kinship relations, and about local views of urban society appeared to be taken as flattering.

The difficulties I faced in conducting fieldwork simultaneously among two somewhat antagonistic groups are probably very common. The solution arrived at by Allison Davis and his colleagues in their study of southern "caste" relations hinged on the placement of fieldworkers in the Negro and white communities separately (Davis, Gardner, and Gardner 1965:xiii). Although my case was different, it is my opinion that I acquired information not available to either local people or those in "the community" and, in doing so, created a minimum of friction and animosity between the two groups. That it was a delicate and taxing operation to keep up good relationships with people in both groups cannot be denied.

The cooperative community receives almost no mention in this book. They have, in my view, had little impact on their mountain neighbors. The exception is the presence in the cooperative community of a physician who treats a number of local people. However, as many people, perhaps more, consult physicians in the surrounding towns. A barrier exists between the mountain people and those in the cooperative, and social relations across the barrier are minimal and quite unlike what occurs among members of either group when left to themselves. Thus, with some misgivings, I have excluded the cooperative from this account. For similar reasons, I have little to say about the "summer people," although their view of mountain people would in itself make a useful study.

My research among the cooperative community members was completed in July 1966, just one year after I began. From then until I left the Little Laurel in August 1967, I gave my attention to finishing the research I had started among local people. In addition to this period, I returned for the summer of 1968 and made a brief visit to the valley in 1972. My account in this book draws most heavily on the 1966–1967 period. Subsequent visits revealed only the working out of changes that had long before been set in motion.

In conducting fieldwork in the Little Laurel, my activities were like those of most anthropologists in similar field circumstances. My daughter attended the local elementary school, and my wife and I participated in many of the usual activities of adults in the valley. We planted vegetables in our garden, made daily visits to different families, got involved in local politics, and in general tried to be "neighborly." My wife became, mostly by default, one of the local Girl Scout leaders and my daughter a member of the troop. We ordered things from the Sears, Roebuck catalogue, made monthly trips to the city of Masonville, and maintained credit accounts at a number of local stores.

For a few months in 1966 I was hired by the local antipoverty organization to teach night classes for adults in eighth-grade level English. This, of course, enabled me to extend my knowledge, and I did not hesitate to assign themes on topics that were of interest to me as well as agreeable to the adults whom I taught. At one point, I was for several days a substitute teacher in the seventh-grade class at the Little Laurel school, where enthusiasm for the textbook was considerably below that of the night school.

Most of my time, however, was spent with local men. At least once each day I would visit several stores in the valley, and sit in on the groups of gossiping men or, if the storekeeper happened to be alone, perhaps attempt to clear up puzzling points about kinship obligations. I found these hours, particularly those spent in the presence of the two or three excellent storytellers in the Little Laurel, thoroughly enjoyable, aside from whatever anthropological usefulness they might have had. At other times, I helped a number of local men gather corn or hay, build sheds, cut trees, pull and pack galax, and search for rich stands of huckleberries. When I needed aid in, for example, repairing frozen water pipes, it was readily and cheerfully provided.

The most trying episode in my entire fieldwork came in the spring of 1966, when preparations were made for the selection of delegates to the county Democratic convention. Shortly after my arrival—too shortly by strict reading of state election law—I registered myself and my wife as Democrats. This declaration of political allegiance did not seem to impair friendly relations with Republicans, many of whom became close associates of my family and me. But I was, quite inadvertently, drawn into the factional conflict among local Democrats in 1966. Being an associate of some men who supported the "reform faction" (see Chapter 8), I was invited to a secret caucus of fourteen men who were constructing a list of potential county convention delegates. During the meeting, as we sat in the living room of an affluent retired New Yorker who was about to make his debut in local politics, each man was asked to choose one person to appear on the list. Each choice was of the man seated next to the chooser, and I, despite my protestations of ignorance and inexperience, was added to the list.

Meanwhile, unknown to me, I had also been selected for the delegate list of the opposing Democratic faction and was astounded when, the next morning, I was informed of this honor. Had the situation not contained such potential for ruin of my fieldwork, I might have reflected on this incident as a sign of my friendly acceptance by people on both sides. My efforts to "straighten out the mess" ran into difficulties. Since the opposition leader's house was in full view of the highway that runs through the valley, I could not risk driving to see him to explain that I had stumbled into circumstances I could not avoid. To reach his house I spent fully half a day sneaking along the riverbank and then, having reached a spot opposite his house, running across the road to knock at the door. He was quite unperturbed about my situation, and assured me that we would continue to be friends.

With others of the "reform faction" I was elected a delegate to the county convention, and was thus able to gather further information about local politics. Keeping a low profile in the months before the election, I soothed whatever ill will had been aroused against me among the Republicans. All in all, the experience was valuable for fieldwork purposes, if a bit harrowing for my nerves.

Other than the family's success in being helpful neighbors, I think that my personal background had a great deal to do with the kinds of information I gathered in the Little Laurel. Certainly my view of life there was very much influenced by what I knew already. While setting down the details of my prior experience would be excessively tedious—would indeed constitute writing my autobiography, a task I am not motivated to take on—I think it might be useful to sketch in some relevant factors.

I was born and reared in the Deep South, in a part of west Florida that is culturally similar to southern Alabama and Georgia. My father, who lived on a south Alabama farm until he was an adult, moved to Florida and became a carpenter. My mother's family, settled along the coast of Florida for several generations, in many ways resembled, as I reflect on it now, the people of the Little Laurel. As I learned, however, there were significant differences.

After serving in the army, I returned to a state university in Florida and went from there to graduate study in history at Berkeley. The final leg of my educational journey was at Illinois, in anthropology. In between these periods of formal education, I held jobs as typist, housepainter, carpenter, archeologist's assistant, and construction laborer. (I found it difficult to tolerate more than two consecutive years of unrelieved student life.) It was the rather varied experience I had, particularly given my anthropological interest—developed long before graduate study in anthropology—that provided immense aid in learning of the people in the Little Laurel. When, for example, there was mention of washpots, I knew from my own experience what was entailed in their use. As a child, I had stood by my grandmother's cast-iron washpot, where clothes were boiled in soap suds, with a "punchpole" to jab the clothes under the water. Until I was twelve, electric lights were a novelty: at home we used kerosene lamps. The staple sauce of Little Laurel meals, "sawmill gravy," was familiar to me as "Hoover gravy," a term bestowed by working-class people like my father who suffered from the Depression and decided on a scapegoat. "Blockade," the clear, beaded product of illegal moonshine distilleries, was the first strong alcoholic drink I had as an adolescent—the quality has been much diminished in the intervening years. All in all, there were many similarities, most of them I must admit only faint echoes, between what I knew as a child and what I encountered in the Little Laurel.

In associating with the men of the Little Laurel, my past labors as a carpenter and construction worker came in handy. More than these specific abilities, however, I shared an attitude with them: that of a handyman, of somehow considering the employment of a specialist—plumber, electrician, mason—as almost an admission of failure. It is assumed by them, and despite everything I hold the same view, that if one has sufficient time and desire, he can build his own house or repair his own automobile, and so on. Not specific acts, but the general outlook that this reflects provided me with a bridge of commonality with my informants.

In first observing the men's discussion groups (Chapters 7 and 8), my reaction was to keep silent. I went to stores, made my purchase, drank a cola, and retreated out of earshot of people. In thus biding my time, I gained a reputation, as I later learned, for not "nosing in on" other people's affairs, for not being too curious. As time went on, I gradually began to sit and talk with the men. Even after many months, however, I listened far more than I talked, as I suppose most anthropologists do. When the young antipoverty volunteers came to the valley, I was appalled to find them doing things that were sure to accomplish precisely the opposite of what they intended. They had no reluctance about introducing themselves (rather than let storekeepers do it for them, after they had retired from the scene), and asking direct questions about people in the Little Laurel. Perhaps it was their impatience to get on with important tasks, or that they thought the valley to be a sort of impoverished replica of urban America that led to this kind of behavior. Unlike many people in the Little Laurel, I do not think it was simple arrogance.

Just before I left the valley, several of my informants went out of their way to assure me that they had already located two jobs for me: at a nearby furniture factory or in a regional church college. There was really no need for me to leave, they said. The sentiment, as far as I could tell, was genuine, and my appreciation equally so.

2 / The Little Laurel: an overview

Since at least 1844, when one of Edgar Allan Poe's short stories mentioned the "fierce and uncouth races of men" living in western Virginia, there has developed an image of people in Southern Appalachia as slovenly, impoverished, ignorant, and sternly individualistic. A British traveler wrote in 1856 of mountain people in western North Carolina:

> The fact is, the people of this whole region devote more of their time to hunting than they do to agriculture, which accounts for their proverbial poverty. You can hardly pass a single cabin without being howled at by half a dozen hounds, and I have now become so well educated in guessing the wealth of a mountaineer, that I can fix his condition by ascertaining the number of his dogs. A rich man seldom has more than one dog, while a very poor man will keep from ten to a dozen (Lanman 1856:400–401).

While the strong bias of these earlier accounts is now muted into earnest expressions of sympathy for people "forgotten" by urban America, Southern Appalachia is still, in the popular view, a land of blood feuds, Elizabethan survivals in folk music and speech, and gaunt, barefoot hillbillies. It is, for urban Americans, something of a quaint survival from their collective pioneer past. In a sense, Southern Appalachia serves as a symbol of an earlier and less complicated era that could produce folk heroes like Daniel Boone and Abraham Lincoln.

Despite the obvious disadvantages of its well-advertised poverty and geographical isolation, life in the Southern Appalachians still appeals to urban Americans. A life now degraded from its former proud height, perhaps, but nonetheless recognizable as part of the common national heritage. Like the cowboy, the hillbilly—of both the Appalachians and the Ozarks—is an American folk symbol. But while the cowboy became the protagonist of high romance, the hillbilly was gradually transformed into such cartoon figures as Snuffy Smith and L'il Abner.

Contrary to what one might infer from the recent flood of newspaper reports and magazine articles about the region, life in Southern Appalachia, or the Southern Highlands as it was earlier known, varies considerably from one place to another. It is a huge region, spreading over 182,000 square miles along the ancient mountain backbone of eastern North America, from West Virginia to northern Georgia. There are, to be sure, similarities between the coal mining towns of West Virginia and the farming hamlets of Tennessee and North Carolina. But, given the tendency in popular accounts to gloss over the differences, these similarities—of values and social organization—receive an emphasis that obscures very real distinctions. Mining towns differ considerably from villages where growing tobacco occupies most of the population. And most public attention has been upon the destitute conditions of mining towns.

This book is about people in one small part of Southern Appalachia: the Little Laurel River Valley in western North Carolina. No valuable coal seams underlie the hills here, and farming as a full-time job is almost unknown. People in the Little Laurel lead a varied economic existence; their social life is a blend of traditional and modern patterns. Many of the characteristics attributed to the people of the Southern Appalachia region are shared by the residents of this valley; some, like the hopeless resignation so frequently considered typical of unemployed coal miners and their hungry families, exist only as faint and uncommon undertones. Only when the region is compared with other parts of the country does poverty become so outstanding a characteristic. Yet, despite the low income of many families in Southern Appalachia, their lives contain much that is satisfying. Neither the magisterial declaration of Arnold Toynbee that the inhabitants of Southern Appalachia are "no better than barbarians . . . a people who have acquired civilization and then lost it" (Toynbee 1946:149), nor the recent contention of an American sociologist that mountain people are "opinionated, dogmatic, and argumentative," and lead a life "emphasizing stereotyped behavior, dependency, belligerence, and fatalistic resignation" (Ball 1971:74–76) seems appropriate to the Little Laurel. So, too, with the clichés of admiration found in periodicals aimed at the urban public, where the mountain people are praised as "the last of the rugged individualists" (Kernodle 1960).

These descriptive epithets, pungent as they may be, miss what seems more significant for an understanding of life in this part of the United States. It is, first of all, a distinctive subculture which shows much evidence of continuing patterns more widely known in nineteenth century America. With the tides of rapid change in Southern Appalachia, especially in the past twenty-five years, has come the adoption of many aspects of urban, industrial life.

THE LITTLE LAUREL VALLEY

The Little Laurel, populated in 1965 with about 1300 persons, is walled in on three sides by high, forested mountains rising to 3400 feet on the east and south and to over 5000 on the west. Forming the western wall of the valley, the Craggy Mountains run northward for about 10 miles before dropping abruptly into another valley. On the south, the Sourwood Mountains, intersecting with the Craggies at Mount Henry in the valley's southwestern corner, close the valley off with a barrier across the southern end. Big Ridge, a spur of the Sourwoods, juts out to the north and stands as a barrier on the east. At its widest point, the valley is about 3 miles across.

The Little Laurel River, falling swiftly from its source on the flanks of Mount Henry, winds northward through the valley and joins another larger stream outside the Little Laurel. Throughout its length the river is fed by numerous creeks,

Looking northwest from the top of Big Ridge, one can see several of the settlements in the Little Laurel Valley.

most of them flowing through narrow bottom lands which are occasionally flooded by the rush of melting snow and heavy rains.

The valley shares with the surrounding area a remarkable variety of flora: the number of species is one of the highest of any region in the temperate zone. Much of the virgin forest—of chestnut, oak, birch, poplar, and several kinds of conifers —was cut away during the period of large-scale logging operations, from about 1900 to 1920. Under the second- and third-growth forest of the present day lies a thick tangle of rhododendron, laurel, and smaller plants. Many of these have been important at various times in the local economy. A few still are, and logging on a very modest scale is even today a significant economic activity for some families.

Together with the exploitation of forest products, the extraction of minerals has provided the Little Laurel people with their main source of cash income. Mica, kaolin, and feldspar are chief among the minerals found here. Small deposits of mica abound and the slopes of the surrounding mountains are pock-marked with abandoned mine pits. Like other economic endeavors, mining was conducted on a small scale, with a three- or four-man crew making up the usual work force for each mine. By 1960 the richest deposits of minerals were depleted, and new techniques of extraction, requiring large capital investment, meant that mining could no longer be carried on by small, ill-equipped entrepreneurs. No large mining company exists in the Little Laurel, but a few men commute to work in the mines of adjacent hamlets and counties.

Commercial agriculture, precluded in earlier times by a lack of paved roads and cheap transportation, is practically nonexistent at the present time, although several tiny tobacco plots are scattered through the valley. Farming of the sub-sistence type traditionally provided a major portion of each family's food; vege-

As with almost all Little Laurel households, this has a well-tended vegetable garden, and a prominently positioned television antenna.

table gardens are still an important resource for almost all households. Even for those who might find a garden economically unprofitable, there is a general expectation that the family will each year plant, tend, harvest, and preserve for the winter a variety of vegetables and fruits. Members of even the most affluent households will generally gather blackberries and wild strawberries in the summer.

The production of household articles—handmade shoes, chairs, baskets, brooms, and so forth—within the Little Laurel has steadily declined as the availability of mass-produced goods has grown. This trend toward the substitution of factory-made items for those once made at home has been brought about primarily by greater access to cash income, through the introduction of small industrial plants within a thirty-mile radius of the valley, and by increased contact with commercial centers. A highway construction program begun in the 1920s and the rapid growth in the number of automobiles owned by residents of the valley provide the means by which families can now reach the nearest urban center (a city of 65,000) in an hour's travel. Before 1930, a trip to the nearest trading town, a distance of 25 to 30 miles over the Sourwood Mountains, required three or four days by horse and wagon.

SETTLEMENTS AND COMMUNITY

The Little Laurel is made up of ten distinct settlements. Each settlement is composed of a cluster of dwellings, perhaps a general store, and one or more churches. Each has a name. Regardless of the settlement in which one lives, he will identify himself to people from outside the valley as being "from the Little Laurel section." The same kind of geographical identification is used throughout the county. People are "from Hardscrabble," "from Painter Gap," or "Split Branch." This extends, in the case of adolescent boys attending one of the two county high schools, to being classified as "Little Laurel toughs," an expression which connotes backwardness, stubbornness, and extreme rurality. This label is only partly accounted for by the fact that the Little Laurel has long been one of the most sparsely settled areas of the county. Until quite recently it was known outside the valley as a place where the making of illegal whiskey thrived, where one could escape capture for evasion of the military draft, and as the location of ignorant and poverty-stricken people.

The geographical boundaries of the Little Laurel coincide with its political boundaries as one of eleven townships in Kent County. The township limits trace a ragged line along the crest of the Craggy Mountains. On its other mountainous sides, the Little Laurel borders two adjacent counties, each of which contains a larger town than does Kent. One result of the improvements in transportation in the past twenty-five years has been to encourage the valley's residents to consider Chesterville, about 15 miles from the valley and the county seat of Kent, as an economic center. Before the late 1940s Chesterville, a town of only 1400 people in 1960, was regarded almost entirely as a center for political activities. Today, families from the most distant parts of the county, including the Little Laurel, gather in Chesterville not only to enjoy the festive occasions of "court day," but on Saturday mornings to shop and meet friends and kinsmen from other areas in the county. For those residents of the Little Laurel who work in the three textile mills in Chesterville, a trip to town is, of course, a daily affair.

Townships are significant political units. Each of the national political parties, Republican and Democratic, has its own political organization within the township, and members of each party hold township meetings to elect delegates to a county convention. At different times in the past, the county's politics have been organized by primary elections and, at other times, by the convention system. Individual votes assume greater importance in the convention system when election of delegates, and thus a voice in the selection of candidates for county political office, can be decided by one or two votes. In primaries, where votes are tabulated for one political party throughout the county, single votes have much less influence in any particular township.

Little Laurel Township also has a registrar of voters, a three-man school committee to make recommendations to the county school board on purely local school matters, and a "tax lister," who enumerates the property of township residents for the assessment of personal property taxes. Appointments to these positions, as to many others which are not specifically political offices, are based on patronage; the party in control of county government, usually but not always the Democrats, insures that local appointees are of the appropriate political persuasion. Township office-holders must not only belong to the reigning political party, but be identified with the faction of their party which has won the recent elections.

Thus, the Little Laurel can be considered both politically and territorially as a community. As we shall see in the following chapters, territory, and the relatively isolated location of the Little Laurel, are far more significant to the residents of the valley than political boundaries.

THE PACE OF CHANGE

To say that the Little Laurel has undergone rapid changes in the years since 1945 seems entirely too mild. There are many older adults who remember, from their first years of marriage and parenthood, loading a wagon for the three-day trip over Sourwood Mountains to trade home-cured pork for salt and flour. As late as 1942, "acid wood" and "tan bark," both used in tanning leather, were being hauled out of the valley to tanneries across the mountains. Similarly, the memory of the painful experience of breaking in a new pair of wooden-soled workshoes, put together by a local part-time cobbler, provides many older men with a reference point from which they can "study about" the changes wrought in their lives in a few decades.

Since the mid-1950s a growing number of tourists has come to the Little Laurel in the summer months. Some, the "summer people," build or buy cabins and spend the entire summer in the Little Laurel. Others come to relax in the campgrounds of the national forest, which incorporates most of the land in the valley. Retired persons, far less numerous than tourists or summer people, make the valley a permanent home. These outsiders, predominantly from Florida but also from Illinois, New York, and New Jersey, have increased from less than ten households before 1955 to over forty in 1968.

Electricity, entirely absent from the valley before 1948, is now available to almost every household. A few homes are still lit with the kerosene lamps once used by all. Local storekeepers maintain a stock of these lamps, selling them to tourists as souvenirs and to local families as necessities. The availability of electric power has led to unprecedented change in domestic labor. Although a number of households lack automatic washing machines, laundromats with coin-operated machines are located within 10 miles. Radio and, later, television have brought urban attitudes within range of the entire valley. By 1958 just over 100 television sets were owned by Little Laurel families, and nine years later the number had swelled to over 200. By that time, 1967, there was almost no one in the valley who did not watch a program once or twice a week.

Telephone service has vastly extended in the valley in these decades. Before an expansion program in the late 1950s, only 5 telephones existed in the Little Laurel. By 1967, the number had risen to 146. All are on four- and eight-party lines; private lines are unavailable.

The frame schoolhouses of the 1940s and before, consisting of one or two rooms and an outdoor toilet, gave way in 1953 to a consolidated elementary school. With this centralization of educational facilities went the addition of paved roads branching off the state highway which winds through the valley. At about the same time, the highway was widened and its dangerous curves straightened to accommodate the increased traffic of tourists and local residents. Automobile ownership grew from under 100 in 1950 to more than 450 by 1967.

But by far the most significant change in the Little Laurel in the years since 1945, as for Kent County as a whole, has been the shift from agricultural to industrial employment. In fact, this change is the basis for the transformation that has come about in this region. From 1930 to 1960 the percentage of the county population holding agricultural jobs declined from 66 to less than 25. In the same period, employment in the textile industry jumped from less than 1 percent to almost 17 percent.

Three textile mills in the county seat, all built since 1945, account for some of this growth, but, in addition, many men in the Little Laurel commute to industrial jobs in nearby counties. A few go as far as Masonville, 50 miles distant, for work. Added to those who return to the Little Laurel each night from jobs 10 to 50 miles away, there are many cases of temporary migration out of the area.

After an increase of population from 1910 to 1940 (909 to 1701) in the Little Laurel, migration out of both valley and Kent County grew steadily and continues at present. This trend has been characteristic of the Southern Appalachians in general. Migration from Southern Appalachia to industrial centers of the North and East, a movement already underway in the late 1930s, thinned the mountain population during the period 1940 to 1960. Kent County's population fell to just over 16,000 in 1950 and to 14,000 ten years later. Loss of population in the Little Laurel was comparable, as we can see in Table 1. In that decade, the county lost 14 percent of its population. Contrary to what people in the Little Laurel frequently say—that "lots of folks leave here, but they always come back, some day"—the valley continues to lose many of its younger families, who seek better economic prospects than the mountains afford.

Leaving the valley in order to get a job is not altogether a new thing. Although the Little Laurel and its people were, thirty years ago, far more isolated than today, there is an established pattern of migrating to other areas for employment or to escape domestic or legal entanglements. This alternative has existed for much of this century, but has been of major significance only since World War II. "Before the war" and "after the war" are common points of reference among the local people, not only in speaking of types and places of employment, but also as a means of noting the disjunction in values, styles of interaction, religious belief, and many other aspects of life. The contrast is between a former period of widespread self-sufficiency on family homesteads and the present, with its proliferation of suburban house types, industrial employment, religious "modernism," and the decreasing importance of kinship as the dominant dimension of local

TABLE 1   POPULATION, LITTLE LAUREL TOWNSHIP*

Year	1940	1950	1960	1967
Population	1701	1540	1388	1304

* From U.S. Census figures and author's census for 1967.

social organization. Relationships with industrial employers, in an atmosphere of routine hours of work, enforced regularity of attendance, and the performance of repetitive tasks, tend to be businesslike and impersonal. The separation of places of residence and employment, too, is a new thing for many men and women in the Little Laurel.

Besides employment in industry, either through seasonal migration or by the rapid increase in industrial plants in this region, the people of the Little Laurel depend more and more on tourism for their income. Tourists now provide local storekeepers with a significant proportion of their business. Trade is brisk in the summer months, and the more ambitious merchants with advantageously located stores have added picnic supplies, small bundles of firewood for campfires, crushed ice, and souvenir trinkets to their traditional stock of hog feed and cornmeal, "fatback" pork, and dried beans. Here, in the contact of storekeeper and tourist, is another area of social life where efficiency and impersonality are keynotes. Summer visitors are usually uninterested in "settin' a spell" in a local store to carry on what must often seem dull and pointless conversations. They quickly make their purchases and withdraw to the public campgrounds or isolated cabins. To attract more customers from among these vacationers, storekeepers pay more attention to urban rules of neatness by keeping the floor swept and arranging goods on the shelves attractively. Self-service has become customary in the larger stores, where much of the summer business is from among the tourists. Yet many local shoppers follow the traditional rule of asking for each item. In those stores where few tourists are encountered, the arrangement of furniture, with a long counter standing in front of the shelves of goods, precludes self-service entirely.

Outsiders add to the growth of knowledge and tolerance for urban mannerisms and attitudes, although much of the breaking down of provincialism appears to be due to television. As local people see the "impossible" repeated as a matter of routine, showing up dramatically in technological feats such as space travel, their doubts about the literal truth of the Bible and the durability of folk wisdom multiply. A rueful comment was made by one troubled man, a firm believer in the tenets of traditional Protestant religion, at the end of a lengthy discussion of the religious reasons no human would ever travel to the moon: " 'Course, none of us ever thought they'd be a highway [the paved road which follows the crest of the Sourwoods] right up there on top of them mountains. Or such a thing as television, either." Nevertheless, when a crew of astronauts was accidentally burned to death, the same man reflected that "it was God's will, it was His punishment, just like them people settin' up a tower [of Babel] to heaven." For that segment of the population who assiduously imitate urban life styles, such doubts are being replaced by disinterest in theological disputation and explanation. They more and more regard the church as a locus for social gatherings rather than as the source of ultimate knowledge.

Throughout all aspects of contemporary life in the Little Laurel, old and new are mixed. A blend of modern and traditional is apparent wherever one turns. Merchandise in the stores will include cast-iron kettles and kerosene lamps alongside the latest version of "instant" food and electric clock. A man clad in blue denim overalls, walking along the highway with a cotton bag (a "poke") of groceries slung over his shoulder, presents a striking contrast to the stream of new automobiles passing in both directions. In some houses, an electric range stands unused beside an ancient wood cookstove. With the introduction of electricity, the new stove was purchased to replace the wood-burning one, but in this instance some women have decided the older way is best.

CENTRALIZATION AND DISPERSAL

Sweeping the people of the Little Laurel closer and closer to the social and cultural patterns of urban America, the changes of the past quarter century can perhaps best be seen as a growth in centralization. Shifting away from the isolation and relative self-sufficiency of its separate neighborhoods, the Little Laurel has become more tightly integrated, its links with the world outside more important.

The school system has been consolidated. Before 1952, five small schoolhouses were in operation in the Little Laurel. In that year, a modern, brick structure was erected. In 1953–1954, two large, consolidated high schools were built near the county seat and students from the Little Laurel in grades nine through twelve began riding buses to East Kent High School. While high school had, before this time, been only 6 miles distant and included no students from the county seat, the new school, 10 miles from the Little Laurel, includes children from five townships. Ninety-six percent of the 500 students ride buses to and from school.

Changes in communications have, besides the huge increase in telephone service and numbers of television sets, resulted in centralization of the postal service as well. The five post offices of the 1930s were housed in the corners of convenient stores, with storekeepers serving as postmasters. Now the entire valley has become a single route, with daily service provided by one man driving his station wagon from box to box.

"Car pools" are organized in the Little Laurel to transport factory employees to work; the numbers of individuals who make their living by taking odd jobs—"hacking around" is the local expression—has greatly decreased. The automobile has also made it possible for families to shop in the county seat and even further away. Local stores find fewer of their customers buying a week's supply of groceries locally; supermarkets in town offer lower prices and larger selections of items. Storekeepers in the Little Laurel rely on other sources of income in addition to merchandising, and tend to hold as regular customers only those who cannot manage to pay cash.

An especially interesting example of the manner in which old and new patterns converge is found in the usual activities following death. Coffins are no longer hammered together by the deceased's family and friends: a mortician furnishes a manufactured casket and embalms the cadaver. Yet, in the traditional fashion, the grave is "laid out" by a local man who has some experience as a surveyor and dug by a group of kinsmen. The mortician receives a fee for his services, but the gravediggers work without pay to fulfill an accepted obligation. Funeral sermons are usually preached in the church rather than in the deceased's home, as was formerly the case. The grave, however, is in most instances located in a cemetery that carries a family name. No payment for the gravesite is required.

Less easily described but certainly apparent to the observer is the rapidity with which the people of the Little Laurel adopt urban styles and measure their life by urban standards. Popular songs pour from the radio stations in the area; "TV dinners" become more and more popular, particularly in those families where the wife is employed; clothing cut in the latest fashion is seen more frequently; sedans, rather than pickup trucks, are preferred by younger families. Profanity is heard more often when men converse. Only one man in the Little Laurel has taken up golf in preference to the traditional sports of hunting and fishing, but serving late-afternoon cocktails to guests, contrary to traditional usage, is characteristic of several households.

It is the elusive matter of style which elicits remarks from many in the Little Laurel to the effect that, as one informant put it, "The war just about ruined this whole country [the mountain region]. It wasn't just a lot of us going out and learning things we never would have got here, but nothing seems right any more. It just ain't as good a place as it used to be, that's all." Others note the "confusion" brought on by migration into and out of the Little Laurel, and remark explicitly about their recognition that traditional standards are no longer firmly accepted: "A man don't hardly know where he stands no more; there don't seem to be anything steady."

After tobacco plants have grown this large, cultivation is by horse and plow to avoid bruising the tender leaves. In the intial stages of cultivation, the ground was prepared by tractor.

3 / The pioneer past and recent change

The shape of history is very evident in the Little Laurel. Not only the generally recognized cultural conservatism, but specific characteristics of present-day life are best accounted for by reference to events in the valley's past. Political divisions, different from those in the eastern part of the state, the ethnic composition of its population, and the absence of large-scale mining or commercial agriculture are outstanding features. The development of these features, along with some economic details about the present era, is taken up in this chapter. Just as important as their history, seen from an outsider's point of view, is the Little Laurel perspective. How those from the valley look at themselves is also touched upon here.

EARLY SETTLEMENT AND THE CIVIL WAR

The Southern Appalachian area was legally opened to white settlement in 1778. Before then, however, a number of colonists had ignored the Proclamation of 1763, which forbade settlement west of the Allegheny Mountains, and established small squatters' farms in the mountains. Whether any white men lived in the Little Laurel much before 1790 is uncertain, but in the census taken that year the entire Laurel Valley, of which the present-day Kent County comprised less than one half, showed 80 families or about 300 persons. As late as 1910 a traveler's account of the region noted that "the wild valley of the [Little Laurel] has as yet few inhabitants, but you will want to go there because . . . the valley . . . is a most glorious wilderness, to be in which gives one a feeling of having escaped."

These early settlers were largely Irish and Scots, who came to the Little Laurel and the surrounding area from eastern North and South Carolina and down the broad Appalachian valleys from Pennsylvania and Virginia. As migration to the west gradually slowed in the decades before the Civil War, the Little Laurel began to be closed off from the rest of the state. Building roads in the mountains was prohibitively expensive. It was not until 1840 that a roadbed was completed through the valley, stretching from the county seat east and southward to the crest of the Sourwood Mountains, a distance of about 20 miles. Ten years later it was extended 14 miles, down the mountainside to a town in the next county. Following the easier trails westward, the later stream of migration tended to bypass the Little Laurel area. Life in the valley grew more and more isolated.

Remarkably homogeneous in ethnic background when it was first claimed by white men, the Little Laurel has retained this characteristic to the present time. It is perhaps too much to declare, as local newspaper writers tend to do, that the county is made up of people of "pure Anglo-Saxon stock," but the proportion of surnames from parts of Europe other than the British Isles is negligible. The county is quite representative of the Southern Appalachian region as a whole, where less than 1 percent of the population today is foreign-born. The inhabitants of the Little Laurel are all Caucasian. Less than 1 percent of the county population is Negro, all of whom live in a single neighborhood of the county seat.

The small percentage of Negroes stems from the historical fact that slavery was of only minor importance here. In 1860 there were only 362 slaves in Kent County, at that time including three times its present area. When a county convention met in 1861 to vote on the issue of whether North Carolina should secede from the Union and join the Confederacy, the count was 576 to 548 against calling a state convention to decide the question. On this issue, as on many others before and since, the votes of Kent County were overridden by those from the more populous and slave-dependent eastern sections of the state. Upon the declaration of war, many of Kent's residents rallied to the Confederacy. A small number refused to serve either side. Loyalty to the Union, however, remained important, not a remarkable allegiance given the frontier nature of the mountain region. Federalism, characteristic of the West, was also strong in the Southern Appalachians.

The sharp differences between eastern and western portions of the state were observed by Frederick Law Olmsted, who traveled through the countryside near the Little Laurel in 1859 and recorded these comments of a mountain farmer:

> Slavery is a great cuss [curse], though, I think, the greatest there is in these United States. There ain't no account of slaves up here in the west, but down in the east part of this State about Fayetteville, there's as many as there is in South Carolina. That's the reason the West and East don't agree in this State; people out here hates the eastern people (Olmsted 1860:259).

But it was not on moral grounds that slavery was abhorred. The important reasons were the dominance in political power it gave to the east and its presumed effects on small farmers. Slave labor, thought to be in competition with free labor, was seen as detrimental to the interests of poor men. In the entire mountain area of North Carolina in 1850 there were less than 4700 slaves. Olmsted noted that.

> Of the people who get their living entirely by agriculture, few own negroes; the slaveholders being chiefly professional men, shop-keepers, and men in office, who are also land owners, and give a divided attention to farming (1860:226).

Immediately before the Civil War started, a long-awaited legislative act to create a new county from the northern half of Kent was passed. The new county, Clayton, had a total slave population of only 65 and, although it furnished a few volunteers to the Confederacy, was more firmly Union—and subsequently Republican—than Kent.

People in both new counties felt the stress of war. Tax rates more than doubled in 1861, jumping from $1.90 to $4.65, with the necessity to equip and uniform soldiers for the Confederacy. The property of Confederate soldiers was exempt from the tax, and Union sympathizers raised loud but ineffectual protests about the inequity. Food and clothing shortages became acute during the war, and special commissioners were appointed to distribute additional funds among widows and orphans of Confederate soldiers. Salt and baking soda were practically unobtainable, and the ash from burned corncobs replaced the latter. Salt came under strict government control. At one point, an epidemic of smallpox occurred in the area, and the sick were quarantined in a special camp set up in a remote party of the county.

Apparently more serious than these troubles, however, were the incidence of desertion from the military and the severe weakening of law enforcement. Deserters roved the county, stealing from families sympathetic to either side. One gang of outlaws, organized by a Confederate deserter, seized the Kent County Courthouse and routed the military recruiters sent to capture deserters. To maintain order, the county court resolved in late 1862 to establish a home military force to safeguard the residents from further looting. As the order read,

> it is unsafe to call any more men out of our county into the Confederate service, all who have lately volunteered or who have been conscripted . . . should be organized into a company for county and state defence; . . . our families and property need their aid and assistance of the men liable now in this county for military service; . . . we will use all our efforts . . . to allow [such men] to remain in this county for its defence and for the defence of the state from the depredations of the Tories [Union sympathizers] and Deserters.

The home militia, however, did little to quiet the bitter conflicts that had arisen among families who had, before war came, been amiable neighbors. Indeed, by summarily punishing robbers and deserters, the militia organization made more enduring the hatreds ignited by war. In a very real sense, the war was in this area a civil one.

The partisanship of that period remains, in a more orderly but still fiercely contested manner, to this day. Charges leveled by members of one political party at those of another draw on incidents that date back to the aftermath of the Civil War, when the division between former Confederate and Union supporters grew even wider. Reflecting the differences in number of slave owners and the consequent differences in support for Union or Confederate forces, Clayton County is today predominantly Republican in its political activities, while Kent County is mainly Democratic.

AGRICULTURE

The soils and climate of the area which includes the Little Laurel are excellent for growing grains and grasses, and are especially suitable for pastureland. During the early nineteenth century, Kent County lay on the route from Kentucky and

Tennessee to the Atlantic seaboard along which hogs, cattle, and mules were driven to market. Stock raising became a chief economic activity in the county. In the 1840s uncleared land sold for twenty-five to fifty cents per acre, while sheep pasture land could be had for one to ten dollars an acre. Cheap land, combined with the fact that stock could be sold to drovers passing through from the west, encouraged the development of cattle and hog husbandry in the area. Young animals were subject to attack by wolves, "painters" (panthers or mountain lions), bears, and wildcats. Wolves were given special attention by a county "wolf tax," levied from 1836 to 1857, and the money thus raised was spent as bounties for each wolf killed. In a few decades, this animal was eliminated from the region.

Grains, particularly corn, were important agricultural products in the period before 1900 and, before 1850, corn was usually distilled into whiskey for transport to lowland regions. The high cost of shipment by horse and wagon made export of corn in other forms prohibitive. By making it into whiskey, farmers in this region could reduce the size and weight of their shipments and, at the same time, turn out a high-profit and readily marketable product. It was, in fact, common practice for farmers in other parts of the United States to convert corn into whiskey, and was almost always done where transportation was difficult and expensive. Horace Kephart, a keen observer of life in the Southern Appalachians, quotes an informant in 1909 as he explained why the illegal making of corn whiskey was so prevalent in the region:

> From hyar to the railroad is seventeen miles, with two mountains to cross; and you've seed that road! Seven hundred pounds is all the load a good team can haul over that road, when the weather's good. Hit takes three days to make the round trip, less'n you break an axle, and then hit takes four. When you do git to the railroad, th'r ain't no town of a thousand people within fifty mile. Now us folks ain't even got wagons. Thar's only one sarviceable wagon in this whole settlement, and you can't hire it without team and driver, which is two dollars and a half a day. . . . Look, then! The only farm produce we-uns can sell is corn. You see for yourself that corn can't be shipped outen hyar. We can trade hit for store credit—that's all. Corn *juice* is about all we can tote around over the country and git cash money for. Why, man, that's the only way some folks has o' payin' their taxes! (Kephart 1922:122–123).

Other crops were those usually associated with subsistence farming: fruits and vegetables, wheat, oats and barley. Wool and milk products—butter and cheese —were also important items in the local economy. In exchange for salt, sugar, and coffee, brought into the region from markets in Georgia and South Carolina, the people of the Little Laurel and surrounding areas exchanged beeswax, cured venison, honey, and dried fruits. Animal pelts, too, were shipped to lowland commercial centers.

In transporting goods out of the mountains, the ordinary practice was for several families to make up a wagonload of commodities, paying about four dollars for round-trip shipment of 100 pounds. A trip to markets in the eastern part of Georgia required from thirty to sixty days travel over toll roads and steeply graded trails through the mountain gaps.

FOREST PRODUCTS

There were other products sent from the Little Laurel beside those of the farm. For well over a century the most diverse sources of income have come from the exploitation of the forests. A large variety of plants and plant products has been collected and sold to local dealers, thence shipped by wagon and, later, railroad to outside markets. Bloodroot (used for dyes), raspberry leaves, spearmint, and liverwort are some plants which were important sources of income in the mid-nineteenth century. Others have, during one period or another, risen in importance only to fall into rapid decline as the supply dwindled or the market for them collapsed. Ginseng (*Panex*), a long tapered root highly prized by the Chinese as an herbal medicine, was shipped out of the area as early as 1837. Collected by many local people, it was then bought by a dealer who drove a horse and wagon from neighborhood to neighborhood. The local dealer dried the roots and shipped entire carloads by rail to Philadelphia and New York, where they were retailed to Chinese immigrants. Some was thence exported to the Far East. A rapid increase in the number of people digging "sang," as ginseng is called in the Little Laurel, led to a shortage in the number of plants; the plant had become economically unimportant by 1900. Like other plants which became salable later, there was no thought given to selective gathering or replacement.

There has been a serial quality to the collection and sale of forest products in the Little Laurel. As one product decreases in popularity or availability, another tends to replace it. Rarely, however, do individual families rely on only one source of income. Blaine Whitson, who was born in the Little Laurel seventy years ago and is still there, pointed to this diversity of sources of cash income: "It seems like every generation of people in this country [the Little Laurel] have something or other to do. Nobody don't ever get rich around here, but not many of 'em go hungry either. There's always something they can pick or pull to get something to eat."

Ginseng gave way to the collection and sale of galax (*Galax aphylla*), a low-growing plant used by florists as background foliage. Galax was first shipped from the Little Laurel in the late nineteenth century; it continues to be economically important to poorer families today. Like ginseng, it was purchased by local dealers, then brought to railroad depots by horse and wagon. Also like ginseng, it was not selectively collected and only its abundance, and low price, has preserved sufficient quantities for the present time.

Some plant products required rather extensive processing. The saps of birch and balsam fir trees, for example, were important sources of revenue in the early years of this century. From both, the sap was collected and then distilled. Birch oil, the final product, was used for food flavoring and required more preparation than did balsam oil, sold as liniment. Birch bark was cut into small pieces, boiled in a cast-iron kettle on an open fire out of doors, and the resulting liquor was put through a simple distillery. As informants in the Little Laurel recall, the only difference between stills used for birch oil and those which turned out whiskey was the addition to the latter of a "worm," a coil of copper tubing. In some cases, a still used for one purpose was easily turned to the other. Balsam oil merely required a "boiling down" process, in much the same manner as the manufacture of turpentine from raw rosin.

Oil of pennyroyal, "penneroil" as it is locally known, was another product of distillation. The pennyroyal plant (*Hedeoma pulegioides*), say older people in the Little Laurel, always flourished in fallow land, fields which had been exhausted for growing crops and were set aside for a few years until fertility returned. With the introduction and widespread adoption of modern fertilizers, the system of allowing land to lie fallow was abandoned, and pennyroyal grew more difficult to obtain and consequently less important economically. It was, in fact, only one of a number of plants, all of less economic significance than ginseng or galax.

Logging has been another source of income which has remained important for at least a century. Until 1850 there were only two sawmills in the entire area (at present, three counties), and the inefficient transportation of the time made the shipment of lumber difficult and expensive. In the latter part of the century, however, a steam-engine sawmill was set up in the Little Laurel and lumber was taken out by wagons. Even then, it was a small operation compared to the lumbering activity of the period 1912–1918, when the Craggy Mountain Lumber Company, financed and owned by individuals from outside the Southern Appalachians, bought thousands of acres of timber land for twenty-five to fifty cents an acre. In six short years, the forests had been cut and the logs sawn into millions of board feet and transported over a specially built, narrow-gauge railway to railroad centers and thence to Northern markets. The lumber company then sold the denuded land for one to three dollars per acre, much of it to the federal government, which established a national forest in the area.

Part of the timber production, particularly for small crews and individual self-employed loggers, went into "tan bark," or "acid wood." Tan bark was stripped from hemlock and chestnut oak trees, loaded into wagons, and brought out to a tannery 30 miles across the Sourwoods, where it was used to tan leather. This continued to provide employment for some families until 1942, but is now an extinct activity. From time to time, in the period from about 1880 to 1940, a number of different tanneries—at one time there were four—offered to buy tan bark.

Without markets, or in the absence of popularity for particular woods, much of the timber was burned to clear land for pastures and fields. Older men recall that their fathers burned acres of chestnut trees as a nuisance; there was no market for chestnut or many other hardwoods at the time.

MINING

Mica mining in this area began about 1870, when sheets of mica were first shipped to Philadelphia. Mica, dug from pits by crews of three or four men (rarely more than seven), was carefully separated from the surrounding rock and cut to precise sizes with hand knives. At the present time there are a number of uses for mica, especially in the electrical industry, where it is used as insulation in armatures, irons, toasters, water heaters, and airplane engine spark plugs. When ground into fine particles, mica is used on roofing materials to prevent sticking, in the manufacture of wallpaper, paint, concrete, and automobile tires. The artificial snow sprinkled on Christmas trees also contains quantities of mica.

The need for mica, also important in making optical instruments, was extensive in World War II: it was required for manufacturing bomb sights and other precision optical instruments. The Little Laurel was one source for mica, and production of sheet mica continued until purchases by the federal government ceased around 1960. Scrap mica, which is ground for many industrial uses, has not been produced in the valley since 1965, when the last mine closed, although the surrounding area still provides a large proportion of the national production of this mineral.

One of the by-products of mica mining, at first considered a nuisance, was

The last working mica mine in the Little Laurel closed in 1965 and was soon over-grown with bushes.

feldspar, a silicate used principally in making pottery, porcelain, and enamel brick and tile. As an abrasive additive, it is also used in scouring soaps and, like mica, in the manufacture of roofing materials. Although the Little Laurel itself has not been the site of feldspar mining, the valley's residents have worked, at various times, in the mines of the surrounding area, and even now a few migrate to other parts of the United States to work in feldspar mines.

Feldspar is bulkier than mica and, consequently, requires a more efficient transportation system to make its extraction economically feasible. The first loads of feldspar, hauled out of the region by horse and wagon, brought only a fraction of the profits turned by mica. Only after 1912, when railway lines were constructed near the Little Laurel, did feldspar assume an important place in the local economy. Yet mica continued to be economically paramount until 1921, when imported mica from India brought about a drastic fall in prices. In that year the value of feldspar produced in the region around the Little Laurel was three times the value of mica. Mica only regained a significant position during World War II, and later in the Korean War, as a consequence of price fixing and stockpiling by the federal government. Today, only feldspar remains significant in the mineral production of the region.

LIFE BEFORE WORLD WAR II

Among residents of the Little Laurel, the opinion is unanimous that World War II brought changes of a kind unknown in the region before. "Before the war," in local conversation, is used somewhat loosely to indicate the several decades from about 1910 to 1940. The effects of World War I, it appears, were primarily those of losing a few young men to temporary service in the military, but otherwise they were insignificant in changing the valley's way of life.

Prior to 1940, people in the Little Laurel lived in frame or log houses, "pole houses" as they are called here, and depended on farming and exploitation of the forest and mineral resources for subsistence. Cash, for purchasing manufactured goods and paying taxes, was acquired from the proceeds of open-pit mica mining —"ground hogging"—, from the sale of animal pelts, and from the collection and sale of forest and farm products. Contrary to what one generally assumes as to the self-sufficient character of life in the Southern Appalachians, even in these years there was considerable linkage to the world outside the mountains. When, for example, mica began to be imported in large quantities from India, where cheap labor ensured a low price, the value of mica produced in the southern mountains dropped within one year to less than 20 percent of the previous year's production. Similar circumstances surrounded the production of plant and forest products: markets outside the region had a determining effect on the amounts of mountain products sold and the prices received for them.

Nevertheless, a high degree of economic self-sufficiency and social isolation was characteristic of the Little Laurel area until after World War II. Extensive cooperation, particularly in economic projects, was a feature of daily life. Barn-raisings and husking bees provided occasions for technical cooperation and sociability until quite recently. This kind of cooperative activity has, indeed, not yet disappeared from the valley. There are still instances of sharing of land and labor in raising corn crops, and in sharing the work and profit of cutting timber. More formally, partnerships between friends and kinsmen exist in such diverse enterprises as storekeeping, construction companies, and exchange of labor in building new residences. More and more, however, as the valley's residents find themselves involved in wage labor in the increasing numbers of factories in the adjacent region, opportunities for such cooperative activity decrease.

The difficulty of hauling agricultural products to markets over the unpaved roads of forty years ago presented an insuperable barrier to the development of truck farming in the valley. Automobiles were a rarity until after about 1950, and horse and wagon transportation was unprofitably slow. With the exception of tobacco—grown by less than half of the Kent County farmers in 1945, and averaging less than one acre per grower—and some use of corn as livestock fodder, agricultural activity was confined to subsistence production. Hogs, roaming the forests for chestnuts and acorns, were an important item in the system of economic exchange whereby a family "settled up" with local storekeepers for up to a year's extension of credit for flour, some clothing, salt, and other necessities not produced in the household. Olmsted (1860) noted the same pattern of fattening swine by allowing them to run loose in the forests until a few weeks before slaughter or sale. Informants agreed that what Olmsted wrote of his observations in 1859 applied to the Little Laurel until well into the 1930s, when the "chestnut blight" decimated the forest:

> It is said that they [hogs] will fatten on the [chestnut] mast alone, and the pork thus made is of superior taste to that made with corn, but lacks firmness. It is the custom to pen the swine and feed them with corn for from three to six weeks before it is intended to kill them (Olmsted 1860:224).

"After the war," when trucks and modern highways made commercial farming possible, industry had penetrated the region and wage labor had become significant in the local economy. To those most capable of profiting from it, farming offered little attraction—it had become a symbol of a backward rusticity most younger men and women sought to escape. The lack of large tracts of rich, level land in the valley, and the increasing fragmentation of landholdings by equal inheritance among the offspring of large families, was another impediment to large-scale commercial agriculture. By 1965, truck farming was engaged in only by two or three men, one of whom came from outside the county to the Little Laurel each spring to rent several acres for growing cabbage. Corn, now the hybrid variety encouraged by large amounts of commercial fertilizer, remains the major crop in the valley and is used mainly as fodder for livestock.

CHANGES IN ECONOMIC PATTERNS

As indicated in Table 2, the most significant changes in Kent County's economic life since 1940 have been the decrease in numbers of workers employed in agriculture and the rise in importance of textile mill work. The occupational pattern of

TABLE 2   OCCUPATIONS, IN KENT COUNTY, 1940, 1960*

Occupation	1940		1960	
	Number of Workers	Percentage of Employed Workers	Number of Employed	Percentage of Employed Workers
Agriculture	2690	61.32	924	24.65
Forest Products	335	7.64	232	6.19
Whole & Retail Trade	177	4.03	421	11.23
Professional Services	192	4.38	251	6.70
Domestic Services	111	2.53	—	—
Mining & Quarries	272	6.20	144	3.84
Building Industries	118	2.69	268	7.15
Textile Mill Products	99	2.26	621	16.57
Other	393	8.95	887	23.67
All Industries	4387	100	3748	100

* From U.S. Census figures.

the Little Laurel parallels these changes. Nevertheless, some traditional occupations, particularly those involving exploitation of the valley's forest resources, remain important for many families. Digging "sang," pulling galax, and cutting "sprays" (branches of dog-hobble, *Leucothoë editorum*) were major sources of cash income in earlier years. Ginseng is now rarely seen. Although the price for its dried roots in 1965 ranged from $25 to $30 per pound, only one local family continues to search the steep hillsides for it.

Gathering galax, and to a lesser extent dog-hobble "sprays," has continued to provide economic support for those who are poorest. As a means of supplementing incomes, it is sought by even greater numbers. Women often spend several hours a week pulling galax to earn money for luxuries they could not otherwise afford.

Galax is pulled by small groups of people, usually kinsmen, and collected in large burlap bags dragged behind the "puller." After a day in the forest, the pullers sort the galax, tie it into bundles of twenty-five, pack the bundles into wooden crates, and sell it to local merchants for $1.25 to $1.60 per thousand pieces. Dog-hobble, which is more time-consuming to gather, brings $3.00 to $4.00 per thousand branches. It, too, is sorted and tied twenty-five sprays to a bundle. This kind of work often engages parents and offspring, the adults gathering by day and the children helping to sort and bundle the plants in the evening. A productive day for an adult galacker will bring in 6000 to 7000 plants. The one-day record, according to informants in the valley, was set several years ago when Ralph Wilson pulled just over 20,000 galax from dawn to dusk. His nearest competitor in the contest brought in less than 15,000 and, it is rumored, used a flashlight in a before-dawn attempt to win unfairly.

Evergreens are shipped, by wagon in earlier times and by small trucks at present, to urban centers in the South. While the price varies, being highest in late

These two children are sorting and counting the day's harvest of galax into bundles of twenty-five leaves.

November and early December (due to the demand for Christmas decorations), there is a fairly constant demand for the products and they continue to be a major economic resource. Fortunately, galax is lighter and less easily bruised in winter, when the plant's sap is down. Bags can thus be more fully packed and more galax carried than in the warmer months.

Harvesting evergreens, far more than farming, has acquired a symbolic connotation. As part of the process of "looking over" a stand of timber before offering the owner a bid, lumbermen will sometimes spend a half day pulling what galax they find: "Ain't no use wastin' all that time in the woods." This work is considered, by local people who earn their living as industrial employees and at various white-collar jobs, the occupation of "backward, ignorant hillbillies." Certainly it is a means of support that appeals to those who are oriented more to the traditional way of life than to a modern, urban middle-class style. The tasks involved in gathering galax and dog-hobble can be begun and ended at the discretion of the individual family, the work is unsupervised, payment is almost immediate, and one need not work among strangers.

It's a good thing [said a local galax dealer] for most people around here to be able to pick up a few dollars whenever they need it. Just go off in the woods for a few hours and bring in three or four thousand galax. Some of the children go galacking after school and make a little money. And they can get their money right now—bring it in here and get paid right off. They like that, people around here do.

Cutting and hauling timber and mining mica and feldspar were, until the late 1940s, the two most important economic activities in the valley. Large-scale mining operations were the exception. Logging, in the same way, was on a small scale and involved groups of less than fifteen persons. Ordinarily, one man would purchase a stand of timber or mineral rights to a tract of land and hire local friends and kinsmen to work it with him. Mica was sold to dealers in the county, thence shipped northward. Timber was hauled to local sawmills (seven located in the county in 1945) and sold. When kinsmen mined or logged together they often shared the profits, frequently giving two shares to the man who had secured the mineral rights or "boundary" (tract) of timber. It was this same man who, when necessary, had arranged for sufficient credit to begin operations. When the crews worked for wages in the mines and forest, as was sometimes the case, the relationship of employer and employee was that of friend or kinsman, the hours of work were variable, and men shifted from one job to another as they "took a notion."

Work in timber continues to provide a living for some local men, but it is seasonal and sporadic employment. The work pattern remains traditional: work crews ordinarily involve a group of kinsmen. When a local man, for example, won timber rights to a large tract of national forest land in 1965 by submitting a bid far above all others, it was generally agreed by those who make their living in cutting timber that he "might *just* come out even" and perhaps make a slim profit only because he and his five adult sons would work together. If he were to hire labor, he would surely lose money. When close kinsmen handle a job together, there is no necessity to account strictly for every hour of labor, since each will receive a share of the total profit at the end of the job. In another case (1967), a group was engaged in dragging out chestnut "soggies" (logs which have lain in the forest for years and are partially rotted), a venture that is profitable only because the recent popularity of chestnut for use in expensive cabinetry has led to huge price increases. The group was composed of three men, two of whom were married to sisters, the other a brother of one of these wives.

Those who, like these three, depend on timber as an economic mainstay must supplement their income with other kinds of work, such as growing and selling shrubbery, working for short periods of time on construction jobs, and using small "bullnosers" (bulldozers) to "push off" (clear) land. To maintain steady employment in timbering it is necessary to become—as several families have—migrant laborers, living in Washington or Oregon from April to November and returning to the valley for the winter months.

In the past few years, cattle raising has once again become a popular enterprise in the valley. This man, once a construction worker in Maryland and Washington, has returned to the valley to become a rancher.

There are more irregular ways of adding to one's income. Hunting and fishing, while providing more pleasure than wealth, are even today a supplementary source of food for a few families in the lowest economic category. Raccoon pelts still bring a dollar each, but it is an expensive method of making money and coon hunting is now recognized as sport. Fishing for the several varieties of trout in the river and creeks puts more food on the table with a minimum of effort. As part of the promotion of the valley as a summer resort and recreation area, the state government stocks the river with trout each month during the summer. Local inhabitants know when stocking will occur and eagerly wait downstream for the fish, their lines baited with whole kernels of canned corn. Within a week the river is virtually emptied of all but the most recalcitrant native trout.

Another economically insignificant but socially revealing method of making a few dollars is now nearly extinct, but for many years provided cash in times of dire need. In order to be hired to fight fires in the surrounding national forest a few local residents would occasionally set fire to the forest. Commenting on this practice, which was stopped in the late 1950s, a forest ranger told me:

Whenever there was a fire down here in the Little Laurel, we'd take the trucks and go back into Stony Branch [a neighborhood of impoverished families] and there'd be men and boys lining the roads waiting to be hired. After it was all over, we'd have an investigator go in there to find out who set it, and nobody knew a thing—just didn't have no idea how that fire got started. We quit hiring from up in there [Stony Branch], and we haven't had near as many fires since then.

HILLBILLIES AND MOUNTAINEERS

The image of the ignorant hillbilly—a Snuffy Smith or Li'l Abner—as the typical inhabitant of the region is strongly resented by the people of the Little Laurel. Complaining of the literary treatment of people in Southern Appalachia, a college youth wrote (1958) in the *Kent County Record*:

> For as long as I can remember, the people of this part of the country have been played up in magazines, paintings, radio and movies as the "Snuffy Smith" type of character, who lives in a one-room log cabin, smokes a corn-cob pipe and drinks his "white lightnin" from a jug. As anyone who has ever visited our beautiful, progressive county knows, this impression is misleading. . . . Certainly, we are all thrilled to pick up a national magazine and find the places and people we know presented in them; but it gets old, after so long a time, to be pictured as a "hillbilly" who goes around barefoot, shooting at revenuers and stealing chickens.

In conversations this kind of comment comes up again and again, especially from those in the Little Laurel who are eagerly trying to shed the marks of the traditional culture and adopt an urbanized style of life. In these remarks there is rarely such pretentiousness as that shown by the editor of the county weekly newspaper, critical of an article in a nationally circulated magazine, when she declared:

> I love to hear the old and middle English words that have survived here. They are perfectly good words that were used by Milton, Spencer, Bacon, and later Dickens, to cite a few. To me, such words are colorful and reflect the influence of our pure Anglo-Saxon ancestry. These words stemmed from the Gothic tongue, and are the earliest literary remains in any Germanic language. My only objection on this score *was* that the [magazine] story made it appear to the rest of the nation that the use of bad grammar is the usual speech heard here. . . . We mountaineers, proud of our heritage and our mountain ways, do not wish to be presented to the rest of the nation as anything other than just what we are. Education, modern culture, progress and community pride are *not* foreign to this area as many have made it appear.

People in the Little Laurel, however, stress other features of their history. They see themselves, together with people from the entire Southern Appalachian region, as distinctive, and readily relate tales of their ineptness in adapting to the expectations of people as geographically near as towns in the South Carolina piedmont. A local storekeeper recalled his disorientation when, hired in 1950 as a construction worker in South Carolina, he inadvertently used the toilet assigned to Negro laborers and was jocularly ridiculed by his fellow workers. "It's interestin'," he said, "the way people act different in other places. I reckon that's why I never left this place for very long: I'm scared I wouldn't know how to act any place else. Been here so long, it's all I know."

Younger men, too, find themselves ill at ease in urban surroundings and feel the pull of home. Three local men left in March, 1966 to accept employment in a Connecticut feldspar processing plant. By the end of May, all three had returned to the Little Laurel, despite their announced intention to make their move a permanent one. Since "all but one of the fellers workin' there was hillbillies—the foreman was a man from Hootowl Creek" (a village less than five miles from the Little Laurel)—it was somewhat surprising to see the three return within three months. One of them summed up his sense of difference this way:

> Oh, I liked the country up there. It looks a lot like this around here. But I just couldn't stand the people's way of doing. I was in this bar one night, drinking, and saw this nigger man cussin' out a white woman. She's his girlfriend, it looked like, but he didn't have no call to cuss at her like that. I just couldn't stand it and almost started a fight there. You see all kinds of things like that up there, niggers and white girls and people all mixed up ever which way. I warn't raised like that, and I just can't stand it—just makes me mad as fire to see it.

In speaking about the past, and the effects of history on present-day life in the Little Laurel, the valley's residents emphasize most frequently the characteristics of personal independence, poverty, and a strong emotional attachment to the mountain region. Poverty is a recurrent theme in even the most casual conversations. This is, they say, the "land of make it yourself or do without." An invitation to dine with a family will often be stated in a joking tone: "You're welcome to eat, if you don't care to take grub [i.e., don't mind eating] like pore folks." These constant reminders of the general lack of affluence in the valley are not intended to serve as apology. Indeed there is an undertone of pride in their statements, especially when they can in this manner obliquely point to their ingenuity in overcoming adversity and lack of economic opportunity.

Personal independence is an attribute that receives constant verbal emphasis. This is, indeed, perhaps the most general comment in the extensive literature on Southern Appalachia, and the opinion of the valley residents is repeatedly reinforced by written accounts in books, magazines, and newspapers. A long-time student of Southern Appalachia expresses the view this way:

> The great silence of the eternal hills and the isolation of lives in these deep mountain valleys would make of these Scotch people a quiet, taciturn, but a courageous and independent people. They were both determining their own destiny and having a large share in determining the destiny of America when they lost themselves in these rugged hills (Weatherford 1955:2).

If not expressed in equally flowery language, the point of view is quite the same among Little Laurel people. Clearly seeing the valley as only a local example of an attitude typical of the entire region, a local evergreen dealer remarked that "People all up and down these mountains are just about the same. All of 'em are real independent people. Won't let nobody tell 'em what to do or how to do it; they do their own way." Asking numerous persons how they decided to cast their vote in political contests, I received the invariable answer to the effect that "I make up my own mind, nobody tells me how to vote." As will become apparent later, however, there are a number of constraints to channel one's allegiances and behavior.

Closely related to the concept of personal independence, perhaps more easily regarded an integral part of it, is the notion of personal and family honor. Weatherford romanticizes this attitude also, but, again, his view is simply a colorful statement of what most Little Laurel residents believe to be characteristic of themselves as "mountaineers" or "mountain people." He writes:

> To this good day a mountain man will stand by you to the last ditch if he thinks you are his friend, but he is not too safe a man to trifle with if he feels you have betrayed either him or his friends.
>
> This regard for family honor often exhibits itself in another marked characteristic—namely, personal or individual honor. Mountain people may be careless enough in handling the truth; but if they give their word of honor, they are not likely to break it. Somehow they make a subtle distinction between a simple false statement and the betrayal of what they call their word of honor (Weatherford 1955:67).

The traditional pattern of work relationships provides a useful illustration of how the intertwined attitudes of personal honor and independence are applied in specific situations. To a large extent, particularly in interaction among the valley's residents, these attitudes still prevail. A man agrees to accept employment in order to "help out" his employer, and he speaks of his job as "helping" rather than "working for" or "being hired by" his employer. He expects the relationship to be carried on as between equals, just as are relationships with kinsmen and friends. An employee feels no compulsion to appear for work every day at a specific hour, work throughout the day, and leave for home at a precise time. With some limitations, he considers himself free to come to work or not as he pleases. In addition, he expects to be given a task and left relatively free to accomplish it on his own. An employer's authoritarian manner is sharply resented and is quite likely to induce the employee to, as mountain people phrase it, "quit and go to the house." A Little Laurel man, explaining his return to the valley to engage in logging work with a group of kinsmen, related his distaste for the ten years of work he had done in industrial construction: "I just never did like for nobody to point his finger at me and order me around—nobody."

Mutual aid, given and received from kin, friend, and neighbor, was an economic necessity in earlier times. "Helping out" a kinsman or neighbor—deriving from the husking bees and other cooperative projects of that former era—has persisted. To maintain the probability that aid would be forthcoming when needed, one had to keep up cordial relationships and to try to prevent the potentially permanent estrangement of those who could be called upon for help.

Industrial work, both local and migratory, has pierced this fabric of reciprocity and presumptive equality without, however, obliterating it. A textile plant in the county seat had to institute measures designed to reduce absenteeism and a high rate of employee turnover. The plant manager explained the difficulties of compelling regular attendance this way:

> You see, the first day of squirrel [hunting] season, most of the men would take off from work. They weren't used to regular hours and showing up for work every day. Then first day of bear season, all the bear hunters would take off. We stopped that. If a man was absent without good reason, he lost his job. We told each man when he was hired that he ought to buy snow chains for his car so he could get in to work in bad weather. Pretty soon the mountaineers got used to it, especially so since the jobs were good ones and good jobs are scarce in this region.

This one-man sawmill was designed and built by its operator, who has a solid repu-tation in the valley as a mechanical wizard. In addition to operating his sawmill, he repairs automobiles, tunes pianos, and restores old clocks.

Any man who quit his job and tried to be rehired at a later date was refused employment.

When this plant was established in 1948, it was thought a paltry thing by local people; a much larger competitor was already providing far more jobs. The important difference, as a woman in the Little Laurel recalled, was in the different management of the plants: the larger was operated by "people brought in here from New York," the smaller managed for the most part by local men. At the larger plant little effort was made to adapt to the local way of giving orders, and within a few years the plant closed. As my informant, who held a job in the larger plant, said,

> They'd just cuss and scream at people all the time. They just couldn't keep any help [employees]. You can't treat these ole mountaineers like that. They'll quit; they just won't take it. I always thought you could get a lot more out of people if you brag on 'em than if you criticize 'em all the time. That's the way I raised my children, and I think it works with most anybody.

"Blacklisting," as used by the textile factory, is not the only method for encouraging regular attendance on the job. A furniture factory in an adjacent county offers a bonus of five cents per hour for workers who are not tardy or absent from work for a week. A dependably punctual worker making $1.50 per hour, for example, can actually increase this to $1.55, or about $2.00 extra per week. A regional branch of a national thread company has a different scheme: in its retirement plan, the company contributes 60 percent and the individual employee 40 percent, but if the worker quits, he forfeits his 40 percent. The entire amount, of course, is paid in installments upon retirement.

Not only in their self-estimation and the existence of distinctive forms of social relationships are people of this area different from those outside it. In language as well, they display their distinctiveness, especially in the use of many words and phrases which seem to have been more widely characteristic of nineteenth century rural America. The county sheriff, for example, is known as the "high sheriff." A number of terms are locally used to refer to illegally distilled whiskey: "blockade" is the most common, but it is also called "that old white whiskey," "white likker," and is less frequently known by words more characteristic of the Deep South, "moonshine" and "white lightning."

Their use of words unfamiliar to the outsider is sometimes recognized by the people of the Little Laurel. Certain shrubs and plants have, as they well know, both local names and "book names." Rhododendron, a book name, is called "laurel," and what outsiders call laurel the mountain people know as "ivy." This distinction is so much a part of local discourse that many individuals, in talking with an outsider, will use both names when they mention either of these plants. In predicting the probability of exceptionally large blossoms on the rhododendron, a man told me: "Them laurel bushes is just loaded down with buds, and some of 'em about the biggest I ever saw. That's what you'uns [outsiders] call rhododendron." Only after I had lived in the valley for six months did these double references cease.

It is often observed of the Southern Appalachian people that their speech is exceedingly concrete in its references and ordinarily lacks the qualities of abstraction and generalization characteristic of urban, middle-class speech. This blanket attribution is excessive, but a striking feature of daily speech is the frequent use of similes. If, for instance, a man's patch of turnips or cabbage is not growing well, it is said that the plants "warn't knee high to a dove." A stingy person will be described as "close as bark on a tree and hit stuck tight," and special condemnation can be expressed by calling someone a "suck-egg dog," the lowest (because disloyal) of animals.

The distinctive conservative cultural tradition fostered in this part of the Southern Appalachians after about 1860 has come under increasing pressure to change since 1945. To denote the wide gap between old and new, traditional and contemporary, the people tend to classify events as occurring either "before" or "after the war." In addition to the use of World War II as a time gauge, many of them see it as both the beginning of a material abundance almost unimaginable in former years and as the threshold of a moral ruin that has swept away the rules and behavior of a slower time. Nostalgia is a sentiment felt, at one time or another and to varying degrees, by almost every adult in the Little Laurel. Whether it is expressed as a sense of confusion or frustrated anger, it is a longing, perhaps insincere, for the past. "It looks like the whole mess [all human relationships] is just all out for what you kin git—there ain't much of the right no more," was the conclusion of a storekeeper. And an automobile mechanic noted much the same sort of change when he said: "Why, I remember hearing my daddy say many a time that So-and-so's word was his bond. Folks was just honester in them times. It wasn't like it is now; you could trust a man to do what he said he'd do."

4 / Kinship and sex roles

The importance of kinship in the Little Laurel Valley is inescapable. It is indeed the central organizing principle of social life. Jobs are acquired through kinsmen, one visits most frequently with kin, and ties of kinship form a central topic of local gossip. As many people in the valley contend, "Everybody in this country [Little Laurel] is kin, somehow, to everybody else." While not entirely accurate, this statement does reflect very well the significance accorded to these bonds. Households from which no kinship tie extends to other valley households are rare. When informants mentioned such households, they felt obliged to provide an explanation: "Old Man Lee come in here with the road-building crew thirty-five year ago. He just liked it and stayed, I reckon." Or: "Lafe Simmons heard about all that galax in this valley and him being the best galacker I ever seen, I guess he couldn't stay away." Almost every adult over the age of fifty can reel off the genealogical connections of large numbers of people in the valley, including links of illegitimacy and illegal marriages (that is, between first cousins). Perhaps more telling a feature than this intense interest in kin relationships is the tendency of people in this valley, as in other areas of Southern Appalachia, to judge a person's character and behavior by reference to his kin ties. What an individual *is* depends only partly on his own actions; to a large extent, he is looked upon as a representative, typical or not, of his family.

FAMILY AND HOUSEHOLD

For urban Americans, the image of the Southern Appalachian family is that of the extended family, with a patriarch sternly ruling a large household of adult offspring and their spouses and children. But this idea is quite at variance with the actual composition of families and households. The basic kin group, in Appalachia as in urban America, is the nuclear family, consisting of husband, wife, and their dependent children. What differs here, in the Little Laurel and its surrounding area, is the emphasis put on maintaining close relationships with an extended network of kin. In an earlier era these relationships outside the nuclear family were necessary for sheer survival, and one's kinsmen could be called upon to aid in a variety of tasks, from harvesting of crops and lending of money and tools to providing emotional support for individuals in times of stress. To

35

some extent, this situation still obtains. That is, the nuclear family in the Little Laurel is not isolated from other kin relations. Enmeshed in this larger network of kin relations, the nuclear family is not expected to stress one set of relationships —for example, those of the husband with his parents—over another. As might be expected, maintaining this position calls for a great deal of diplomatic tact and leads to frequent visiting and interaction with parents of both spouses.

The ideal composition of a household in the valley is the nuclear family. But the actual range of households is quite wide, from the separate dwellings of elderly individuals, widows and widowers, to those where the nuclear family is augmented by the addition of various other kinsmen. One household consists of an elderly bachelor, his deceased brother's widow, and this woman's nine-year-old grandson. The boy's mother has divorced his father and remarried; she and her second husband live seventy-five miles distant. Another household, statistically unusual but not regarded as abnormal, is made up of a middle-aged man and wife, their unmarried daughter, and her illegitimate son. Household makeup and size change, with seasonal migration of adult males and their return, with temporary additions of kinsmen for a number of reasons, and so on. A fairly common pattern, as a nuclear family goes through the cycle of rearing children to adulthood, is for the youngest child to remain in the parents' household. Apparently, judging from informants' recollections, this was far more common in the early years of this century, but some households are still of this sort. More frequent is the situation in which a young husband is temporarily away from the valley—for periods of several weeks or months—and a kinsman moves in to "protect" or "help out" his wife. A similar pattern occurs for some households in the winter, when a married daughter (less frequently a son) who has moved to a different neighborhood from that of her parents will return to live with them for the season. This occurred in four households during the course of fieldwork; in only two did the daughter's husband accompany her, but visiting between the households continued.

KINSHIP OBLIGATIONS

The obligations of kinsmen to each other are variously interpreted, but certainly, as informants repeatedly told me, one "ought to stick up for his kin before anybody else." The ideal behavior towards kinsmen, in other words, is based on loyalty. As this ideal is applied to concrete instances of behavior, discrepancies arise, but individual cases of disloyalty can, and are, usually explained by reference to specific events in the past. Long-standing grudges between kinsmen, for example, are widely known and are used as explanations for failure to act in the ideal manner.

In the economic sphere, the general rule of loyalty to kin means that one should patronize stores owned by kinsmen and should not cheat them by charging unfair prices or shortchanging. Kinsmen are expected to, and often do, sell land and automobiles at lower prices to their relatives than they would to nonkin. Cooperative projects frequently are limited to kinsmen, or kinsmen are asked to participate in such projects before others. For instance, when three Little Laurel men decided, separately, to buy whole beefs one winter (1966), they each asked their relatives if they wanted to share in the meat, if they would like to "go halves on a beef." In the case of people who make most of their income from pulling galax, the expectation is that they will share, at least with their close relatives (for example, brothers and brothers-in-law, parents), knowledge of the location of especially rich growths of galax. Direct economic competition between kinsmen is also considered somewhat disloyal. If two brothers both operate grocery stores, for example, they are implicitly requiring their kinsmen to decide to trade with one or the other, and thus inviting conflict among kin. Understandably, situations of this sort of "forced choice" are infrequent, but less divisive instances occur as a matter of course.

Politically, too, one is expected to support one's kinsmen as far as possible. Again, as in the economic realm, one should not run against kin in elections and one is expected to vote, if not actively campaign, for kinsmen in political contests. To illustrate: When Henry Bradshaw announced that he would seek the Democratic party's nomination for county sheriff in 1966, there was general agreement among men in the Little Laurel that, as one expressed it, "if Henry gets nominated, he can't help but win. Why, there's Bradshaws all over this county and he'll get ever one of their votes."

By the same token, only the most extreme provocation leads, or should lead, one to "law"—bring to legal contest—one's relatives. Conflicts that in an urban area involve police and courts can often be settled in informal ways in the Little Laurel. Men hiding in the valley to evade the military draft, as a few did in both world wars, those who are known to make and sell illegal whiskey, and "bootleggers," selling beer and tax-paid whiskey in the county, are protected to some extent by the silence of their kinsmen.

Less easily stated in specific terms are expectations of a somewhat different kind. These include the ideal that parents will not favor one child over another. This is fulfilled by equal inheritance of property in many cases, but by larger inheritance for the adult child who remains at home to care for elderly parents. Grown children should either live in the Little Laurel, although not necessarily in the same neighborhood as their parents, or, if they leave the area, they should return for reasonably frequent visits. Aged or infirm parents should be cared for at home or in the homes of their children.

The diffuse nature of kinship obligations sometimes appears quite dramatically in circumstances when individuals feel a conflict in their responsibilities. Many tales are told about such contradictory moral "pulls." Fate Fairfield, a fifty-year-old logger, recalled such an instance:

We's loggin' up the river on a boundary [tract] of timber and hit started in to rain, so we all got down in under a big ol' rock for shelter. We's settin' in there a hour or two, playin' cards and passin' a bottle of that ol' white likker around. The whisky run out purty soon, and Ransom Wilson—he's the illest [bad-tempered] feller you ever seen, anyhow, even if he *is* my uncle—looked over at somebody else and said, "You called me a sonofabitch!" The other feller said he hadn't, of course. It was just Ransom's imagination all fired up with that likker.

Well, Ransom grabbed the likker bottle and started to hit the other'n with hit, and I grabbed the bottle and told Ransom that nobody hadn't called him no names. Ransom's hand went in his pocket quick as you please. He's after his knife. Hit looked like he was goin' right on and pull out his knife and I was into hit! I had to stop him but he's my uncle, so I just didn't know what to do. Well, Ransom just kept his hand in his pocket and stood there shaking for a while, mad as he could be.

Ransom stayed sulled up [sullen] at me for a long time after that. One Sunday, I guess hit was a month or two after that, I was drunk and went up to his house and told him I didn't mean to make him mad that day. He said, "Ah, Fate, I done forgot about hit. Don't [you] think no more about hit." But I knowed he hadn't forgot hit neither. He didn't act sulled up at me no more, though.

Incidents like this can easily become the focus for years, even generations, of hostility and lead to entire segments of a kinship network avoiding each other.

When one makes critical remarks about kinsmen, as Fate did in the story above ("illest feller you ever seen"), it is almost always followed by a comment intended to acknowledge the kinship link and, by implication, provide notice that one recognizes that he is failing to live up to the behavioral ideal. One very often hears, in cases of this kind, expressions of the form: "I don't care if he *is* my cousin, he didn't have no call to [do so-and-so]," or "He's my sister's husband, but he ought not done that." Remarks of this kind are almost never aimed at an individual's parents, children, or grandparents, although siblings share the immunity with less frequency. This pattern reflects the variable weight of kinship obligations which, while pervasive throughout a wide network of relationships, are stronger as they are nearer ego.

Personal conflicts of loyalty are likely when marriage joins individuals from families of opposing political allegiances. To prevent unpleasant argument, a wife in mixed unions will often register as an Independent, and thereby avoid siding with either husband or father against the other. It is thus possible to agree, to some extent, with both spouse and parent on the occasion of hot political partisanship or at least keep a judicious silence. It is a practice also used by a few men, and for the same purpose: to avoid intrafamilial argument and hostility.

Exceptions to this tendency to preserve peace within the kin group often become the basis for tales repeated over and over for many years. I heard the following story several times from different people, and each time it evoked loud laughter. Harv McIntosh, a prominent Little Laurel storekeeper, was a member of a family widely known as "strong Republicans." When, thirty years ago, he married a woman from a family with the reputation of being among the staunchest supporters of the Democrats, it was expected that she would either take on the political beliefs of her husband or not become involved in political contests at all. But she was a defiant, well-educated woman, a local schoolteacher, and refused to give up her Democratic partisanship. In election after election, for over twenty years, they would, as one man told the tale, "fight like cats and dogs before an election, and then go up there to the polls and cancel each other's vote out." Finally, they agreed to "sit out" one election and forego campaigning or voting. "But ol' Harv just couldn't let it go, and he lit out for the polls along about closing time and voted. Well, the word naturally got back to Lucille, don't you know, and she wouldn't even talk to Harv for more'n a year. That was a awful quiet house."

Kin relationships do not always appear as harmonious and well-integrated as the ideals of behavior would lead one to expect. A man who refused to buy groceries from a store partly owned by his cousin and whose brother, another storekeeper from whom he refused to make purchases, had not spoken to him for over two years, nevertheless stated with great conviction that "you let somebody outside the family jump on me and they'll [kinsmen] come arunnin'. They'll help each other out when things come to a pinch." His storekeeper-kinsmen considered this man a petty thief and were not put out that he did not trade with them. But, when I asked if his expectation of aid in times of dire need was likely to be met, both reluctantly agreed: "You just can't help but do whatever you can for your kin, no matter how sorry they be," said the cousin.

STABILITY AND CONTINUITY

Given the constant talk one hears in the Little Laurel about personal independence and individualism—"Don't nobody tell me how to vote," "People around here just don't take orders, that's all they is to hit"—it seems somewhat incongruent to find the strong sentiment that places persons firmly in the position of representative of a family. It is only partly a belief in the genetic inheritance of personality characteristics that accounts for this pattern. More significantly, it appears to be a belief in the continuity arising through generations of similar patterns of socialization. From father to son, mother to daughter, it is tacitly assumed that children will become, through childhood training and family loyalty, replicas of their parents. If a person belongs to a kin group generally regarded as honest, then the person himself, until evidence proves otherwise, is presumed honest. Although, as one might expect, this does not always turn out to be the case, exceptions are not, it appears, sufficient to bring about general disregard of the rule. In 1965, a truck farmer from Kent County came to the Little Laurel to rent several tracts of land on which to grow cabbage. He promised to pay rent for the entire growing season after he had harvested and marketed the crop. Since, in the words of one woman who rented him land on these terms, "he came from that set of Lewises on Rabbit Creek, I knowed he'd be good for the money, and I let him put out his cabbage on five acres of mine." After the cabbage was packed and shipped out, however, nothing more was heard from the man, either by this woman or others whose land he had used. This did not, nevertheless, appear to diminish their faith in the honesty of the Rabbit Creek Lewis family; the farmer-tenant was considered an exception.

Evidence of specific actions tells also in the case of individuals from families regarded as dishonest. While crediting him with being agreeably different from his kinsmen, Little Laurel people nevertheless express surprise at finding members of the same kin group not sharing the same characteristics. One family in the Little Laurel, the Bradshaws, is the subject of much gossip, and a series of incidents occurring over many years has built for one man in the family a reputation as, in contrast to his kinsmen, unusually generous. Four Bradshaw brothers live in the Little Laurel Valley; three are considered, as one victim of "sharp trading" at the hands of one of them, said, "a gang of thugs—you wonder how a man as honest as Tom [the fourth brother] could come out of a family like that." According to this informant, the Bradshaw brothers not only cheat nonkin, but each other as well. When their father lay on his deathbed, he

> gave a bag of money to Tom and told him to make it to the bank and put it in [deposit it] to his own name. You know, the old man wanted to do a little something extra [beyond equal inheritance] for Tom, he being the onliest one to take care of him when he was sick.
>   Well, I'll tell you, Tom was so scared—he hadn't never seen that much money in his whole life, didn't have no idea his daddy'd had that much. So he asked Will to take it to the bank and put it in for him. Ol' Will did just that: took it to the bank and put it to his *own* name—Just up and stole it from his brother like that.

Numerous instances of the generosity of Tom Bradshaw are given. In each account, he is singled out as an exception among the four brothers and the tale invariably ends with a comment of mystification at Tom's distinctiveness. An informant who grows and sells Christmas trees and other shrubs related the following example.

> I went down to Tom's house one day to see that dang bear he had in a cage and we got to talking about his chickens. Me raisin' bantys [Bantams] like I do, I was admirin' how big his chickens was. He just retched down, grabbed up one, and give it to me. Wouldn't take a cent for it, neither. Well, it was a few weeks after that, when Tom wanted a Christmas tree, asked me if I had any. Told him, yes, come on up to the house and get one. Well, boys, I wanta tell you, Tom come with a chicken in one hand and a poke [sack] full of hog meat in the other. Said, "Henry, I just wanted to bring you a better chicken this time than that 'un you got from me." So we went out there and got him a tree and then I'll be damned if he didn't try to pay me for it. Now that Tom's the best-hearted feller you could think of—and honest. I just wonder how he come out of a family like that.

The requirements of political office frequently conflict with the demands for loyalty to one's kin. It is expected, for example, that elected officials will appoint kinsmen to local government jobs, but a balance must be struck between the duty to kinsmen and the duty to political office. The position of county sheriff, an especially powerful office with the authority to appoint persons to such relatively well-paid jobs as deputy and jailer, is used to further the interests of kinsmen. But the Democratic incumbent of this office was defeated for reelection in 1966 because, according to informants in the Little Laurel, he had not exercised sufficient control over his brother, a deputy, when he had severely beaten an innocent man. "Of course, his brother was older than him [the sheriff]," said one man, "but it still warn't right for him to be bossed around by a deputy." Although a better explanation for the sheriff's political defeat was probably the immense popularity of his Republican opponent, the conflict between bureaucracy and kinship is well expressed.

In the more ordinary situation, an individual acts in the place of relatives, particularly for purposes of "listing taxes"—reporting ownership of personal property—and voter registration. Each year in January, a person in the Little Laurel is chosen by the county tax collector to list taxes for the township. The appointment is made with due regard for political allegiance—if the county government is Democratic, the township tax lister will almost certainly be a firm Democrat—and for availability and need. That is, the tax lister must give a good deal of time to his job during this month, and the appointee is usually an unemployed person with a family to support.

After spending a day or two at each of the main stores in the valley, the tax lister then sets up office at his residence, where he continues to accept reports of property ownership for the specified period. Long spells of inclement weather usually result in a two- or three-week extension of the time period, and consequently more income for the tax lister, who is paid a daily fee. Legally, individuals must list their taxes in person and sign a statement guaranteeing a true and honest statement, but this requirement is not strictly, or even consistently, applied. The tone of the sessions between tax lister and property owner are highly informal. With the exception of the valuation placed on automobiles and tractors, both of which are attached to the property statements before they are placed in the lister's hands, there is much leeway in the interpretation of how the tax law applies. While the printed statement has long columns of such appliances as vacuum cleaners, washing machines, and television sets, rarely does the lister include these items. Television sets are valued at the lowest rate allowable, the lister often juggles figures on furniture valuations, and it is unusual for a family to show more than a total of three hundred dollars, all of which is exempt from taxation.

In my observations of the listing procedure in 1966, the tax lister in most cases aided the owner in deprecating personal property. For example, an owner said of his sewing machine "Hit's just a ol' thing we don't even use nomore. I don't reckon it's worth five dollars," and the lister replied, "Well, let's just skip it then." Item after item is treated in this casual fashion. But if, as happened a few times in 1966, an owner foregoes this back-and-forth process of enlisting the aid of the appointed official in assuring a low valuation, he is very likely to be assigned something approximating the actual market value of the item. "When a man comes in here tellin' me he ain't got nothing worth listin' or his television set's been broke down for a year or somethin' like that, I most always know if it's true or not. If he's tryin' to cheat, I stick him," was the summary statement given by the lister.

Adult sons and daughters very frequently list taxable items for their parents, and sign the parent's name to the statement. Items that are jointly used by an adult child and the parent can be shifted from one tax list to the other to bring about the desired outcome of as low a tax bill as possible. A son and/or daughter can claim as their own some item belonging to their parents, thus decreasing the parents' taxable property. Or, when their own list is unavoidably high, as it would be if they owned a new automobile, they may, with the acquiescence of the lister, shift "ownership" of washing machines, hunting dogs, and other items onto their parents' tax statement. It is assumed in these "negotiating sessions," that the absent persons, usually but not always the parents, will agree to the property shuffling if questions ever arise. This seems to be a generally accurate assumption.

Registration to vote is a process carried out in much the same manner. At announced periods, the "books are open," and qualified applicants can register themselves as voters and as members of particular parties, ordinarily Democrat, Republican, or Independent, in that order of decreasing frequency. Since during the period of fieldwork the township registrar was Democratic, there was a noticeable tendency to be lenient with the requirements if the applicant for registration was known to be a Democrat. Husbands often "signed" the registration book for themselves and their wives; occasionally wives had their husbands added to the list. Adult sons and daughters who lived out of the state, especially those men serving in the armed forces, were listed as voters upon application by their father or mother. Republicans frequently found themselves forced to go through the process in a rather more official fashion, with the registrar administering the legally required oath and accepting only personal applications. Occasionally, when the registrar set up office in the Little Laurel school building, bystanders included Republicans and Democrats and the rules of raising the right hand and taking the oath were uniformly enforced. Most of the time voters registered at the home of the registrar, however, and the procedure was extremely informal.

What is of significance in these two similar situations is the ease with which legal requirements are put aside and kinsmen are allowed, and expected, to represent each other. One time, indeed, the tax lister remonstrated with an old acquaintance, an elderly man in poor health, that he need not have come in person to list his property, but should have "sent that boy of yourn, Bud." The implication until the lister was corrected by the old man, was that Bud was at fault in not insisting that he stand in his father's place: "He wanted to come for me, but I hain't been down here for a long time and I told him I'd come myself."

MALE AND FEMALE

Women in the Little Laurel are expected to have the household as their main sphere of interest and activity. Cooking, cleaning house, and tending to small children are regarded as appropriate daily activities for women and not for men. Interests outside the domestic realm are considered to be the primary concern of men. Such activities as hunting and fishing, loafing in stores, and heavy manual labor almost never involve women, except in the most peripheral way. When, for example, a husband and wife are building themselves a new house, the wife might perform light construction tasks. Gardening, an important part of spring and summer daily activity in the valley, is carried on by both men and women. It is as common to see women of all ages hoeing and weeding vegetable gardens as men and boys. (Products of vegetable gardens are prepared by women, not only for immediate use, but by canning and freezing for storage.) Flower gardens, however, are almost exclusively the province of women, although men deal in shrubbery and ornamental trees and engage in the tasks of caring for this kind of plant in their own yards.

Both men and women participate in some activities, driving automobiles and pickup trucks, and shopping in local stores, for example. Women do not operate heavy construction equipment or large trucks. One interesting exception is the pattern of members of the high school girls' basketball team obtaining jobs as part-time school bus drivers. This situation is a result of the high school principal's partiality in rewarding student athletes with jobs. People in the valley do not regard females driving school buses as inappropriate.

Within the household, women have a great deal of explicitly recognized authority. The care and training of small children, male and female, and older girls is largely in the hands of mothers. Tension between the demands of father and mother most often develops in the case of boys of about the age of eight to adulthood, when mothers try to treat boys much as they do girls, and fathers tend to be more lenient toward the activities of sons of this age. That is, a boy's mother generally expects him to remain at home and spend less time with his peers than does his father, and arguments sometimes arise over these differences.

It is as a moral force, as keepers of traditional moral rules, however, that women stand out within the family and community. They are expected to, and do, attend church more than men, and they take the rules of fundamentalist Christianity more seriously as guides to daily action. Younger women receive no condemnation for smoking cigarettes, nor older women for using snuff, but their position with regard to alcoholic beverages is far more rigidly prescribed. They are considered as "watchmen" over the morality of their households, and it is assumed that women neither drink nor allow drinking in their homes. Kent County is legally dry, and no alcoholic beverages, even beer, may be legally sold in this or adjacent counties. Nevertheless, alcoholic drinks are readily available from a number of bootleggers or by simply making a trip to the state-operated liquor stores in Masonville. Liquor and beer, however, are neither kept in the home nor drunk there. The exceptions are those two or three families who consider themselves "modern" (and, of course, the households of "outsiders"). Even in these cases, liquor is brought home secretly, so "the children won't know," as one housewife told me. By far the more customary procedure is for men to hide bottles of whiskey and cases of beer in the woods and to drink it there with their male companions. Drinking, in other words, is a highly secretive activity in the valley, and is quite generally thought to be "sinful." Cursing, or "blackguarding" as it is locally known, is also a male activity and should not be carried out or condoned in the presence of women or small children.

Of course these behavioral rules are in the nature of ideals and numerous exceptions to them occur. They apply more readily, both in expectation and fulfillment, to people in the middle economic range, where the husband usually has a relatively steady job, either as an entrepreneur—cutting and selling firewood or timber, operating a store, buying and selling shrubbery—or in a factory. For families who depend on the collection of galax or dog-hobble for much of their income, and who are found in the lower income range, the activities of men and women are far more similar. These poorer families commonly constitute a cooperative team, with husband, wife, and older children gathering forest plants, and the entire family preparing the plants for sale in the evenings. Women of poorer families, too, are more apt to be seen fishing and, more rarely, hunting for small game.

Among the few families in which husband and wife have attended college or had extensive experience in urban life, the pattern of strict separation of male and female tasks is also less evident. These people include schoolteachers (male and female), families with both spouses employed in industrial jobs, and younger couples who consider themselves "modern" and whose behavior in most respects is similar to what we expect of a small town middle class. Nevertheless, most people acknowledge, in speech and behavior, the difference between males and females, even if their acceptance of the traditional roles varies considerably. Exceptions, in this wide, middle-economic range, are explained by reference to individual circumstances and peculiarities.

The Harrison family, a mother and five adult sons, is an illustration of exceptional circumstances and persons. Hannah Harrison's husband died when the oldest son was only twelve, and she refused to accept any but the most minimal economic assistance. It is regarded as truly remarkable that Hannah was successful in rearing her sons, all of whom have, as adults, turned out to be hard-working, respected businessmen. Two separately own trucks and buy and sell shrubbery, and a third is a skilled construction worker. All have families of their own and live in new brick houses. The Harrisons are frequently cited as an exceptional family, and much stress is put on the role of Hannah as a "strong woman, as independent as any man you'll ever see."

A much younger woman, Brenda Jackson, is another female singled out for special comment in the Little Laurel. She is the mother of an illegitimate son, whom she has supported since his birth by working in textile mills. Living in her parents' household, Brenda commutes 30 miles daily to and from her job. She is considered an unusual case less for her illegitimate child than for her outspokenness about her ability to provide for herself and the boy. In jocular boasts, she tells acquaintances that "I don't ask anybody to put snow chains on *my* car; I do it myself," and "I make my money, and I spent it like *I* want." Regardless of her obvious independent spirit, Brenda is entirely traditional in her abhorrence of drinking and insistence upon religious training for her son.

Children are treated differently according to sex. Girls have fewer opportunities to associate with others their own age in the absence of adults; far more of their time is spent with parents and grandparents. They are rarely allowed to go on camping trips, and when they do it is under such highly supervised circumstances as in Girl Scout camps. Even here, their mothers tend to be especially watchful, sometimes being repaid with irritated outbursts from their twelve-year-old daughters for hovering about with concern for possible injury. The bond between mother and daughter is expected to be a particularly close one, an expectation that is met to a surprising degree. Adolescent girls attend church and Sunday school classes more frequently than boys, and the vacation Bible schools organized by the larger churches as a summer activity are disproportionately female.

Boys are regarded as more venturesome and likely to take physical risks, and these characteristics are usually encouraged by their fathers. When an informant's seven-year-old son, for example, asked to be allowed to operate his father's power lawnmower, the father immediately acceded to his wishes and began to teach him how to start the engine and guide the mower. Meanwhile, the boy's mother stood on the porch insisting that the work was too hard, that the boy would become overheated, that he would cut off a foot, that he was simply too young to operate dangerous machinery—all to no noticeable effect on the training session taking place 20 feet away. On another occasion, a man had been feeding birds in the winter and standing at his window killing blue jays—"they just steal ever' bit of corn I put out there"—with a rifle. His son, nine years old, wanted to try his hand with the rifle, and the father obligingly taught him how to hold and fire the gun. This kind of behavior is not unusual; it would be a rare boy in the Little Laurel who had not learned to shoot a rifle by the time he was twelve. The first day of squirrel-hunting season teachers in the elementary school expect to find the girls sitting in their seventh- and eighth-grade classrooms. In the autumn of 1966 only one boy in these two grades came to school on that day.

Girls and boys both fish in the valley streams, although girls usually do not do so alone. They sit on the riverbank with their brothers or, less often, in an all-female group.

From the time they are eight years old or so, children are expected to have chores in the household. Some children, in poorer households, are spending entire days in the forests at this age, and put in several hours a day pulling galax. One night, a woman and her seven-year-old son came into a local store to sell several boxes of galax. As the bundles of galax were counted and the mother paid, she handed the boy two quarters as his share, and commended him as a "hard worker." A few minutes later, when he tried to pay for his soda and candy, she insisted that he keep his "wages," and allow her to pay. In a manner that is quite typical for boys of this age, he brushed aside her money and demanded that he be allowed to pay. She finally, with great hesitation, assented to his demand. Girls of similar age perform the usual household tasks: sweeping, making beds, cooking, and washing dishes. Boys chop firewood and carry on activities like those of their fathers.

Regulations about coming home at certain hours are sporadically enforced, when rules exist, for boys and much more consistently applied to girls. Certainly there are exceptions, but they tend to bring the unexceptional into high relief. A family in the Little Laurel which is noted for its urban manner once punished their sixteen-year-old son for arriving home fifteen minutes late by forbidding him to use the family car for a week. This was discussed in several conversations between local men and adolescent boys as, in the words of his uncle, "being too hard on the boy. He just ain't allowed to be like his buddies." The same boy, receiving a C on his high school report card and expecting punishment from his parents for the low mark, was aided in forging the mark to a B by a local storekeeper, who thought that boys shouldn't be punished for making low grades.

Neither boys nor girls spend much time alone. They are almost always in the company of their friends, kinsmen, or both. Constant association with others is so customary that an individual who does manage to be by himself for any period of time is regarded as "quare" and inexplicably eccentric. A seventeen-year-old boy gained for himself the reputation of being, as one of his friends said, "spooky, weird" by borrowing the family car, driving to a laundromat or café in Chesterville, and sitting by himself. His penchant for quietly sitting and observing passersby was mentioned to me time and again by adolescent boys as decidedly abnormal. Finding his behavior unexceptional—he actually spent a small proportion of time entirely alone—I suggested to my young informants that perhaps he was an "independent mountain man." Independence, in their view (as it was expressed to me), did not mean being alone but was an attitude of nonauthoritarianism, a refusal to obey peremptory orders or demands.

SEGREGATION BY SEX

To observe that individuals in the Little Laurel are rarely alone does not imply that there are no restrictions on their associates. Segregation along sexual lines is, by urban American standards, quite marked. This tendency is observable in most daily activities in the valley, as well as in the somewhat more formal events of political meetings and church services. But leisure activities are perhaps most obviously carried out among the sexes separately.

Churches in the valley contain two ranks of pews, with an aisle between them. With the exception of a few young parents with small children, men and women do not sit together during church services: men congregate in the pews on one side, women in those on the other. Small children generally sit with their mothers, and adolescents follow the adult pattern. This sexual separation extends to the knots of worshippers who spread over the church steps before and after services, gossiping, smoking, and exchanging pleasantries. Sunday school classes, held in the larger churches before regular worship services, are also separated according to sex, as well as age. Married men, for example, come together to discuss an assigned Bible lesson in one room or corner of a larger room, while married women meet to talk about the same issues in another room.

Political gatherings and meetings of voluntary associations—for example, community improvement clubs—follow a less rigid version of the same pattern. Here, however, there is a tendency for women of voting age to sit beside their husbands, where they can carry on whispered discussions about how they should vote or can be quietly nudged to follow their spouse's voting inclinations. In less traditional contexts, such as meetings of the local Parent-Teacher Association, the customary separation is not as obvious, although the tendency (if one counts heads) is still present, with women constituting by far the bulk of the audience and a group of husbands seated off to themselves in a group.

But it is in the ordinary round of daily life, occupational, domestic, and especially leisure, that men and women associate most noticeably with those of their own sex. Again, the extent of segregation depends upon the context, upon the content and purpose of specific activities. Women are seldom seen "loafering" in public, while men frequently engage in this activity, in stores, near voting booths on election days, around gas stations in the county seat. In a manner reminiscent of earlier pioneer days, small groups of men gather outside the county courthouse on Saturdays, examining each other's pocket knives and gossiping. Woman-to-woman conversations usually take place on porches and in house yards, and usually among close kinswomen. There are, to be sure, occasions on which men and women join in conversation, the most ordinary being visits of kinsmen on Sunday afternoons. Yet, even at these times, there comes a time in the general conversation at which men draw together on one end of the porch, or wander off to "look at the sow," or "walk out to see Papa's boxwood." That is, the sexual separation is evident even among members of the nuclear family, despite the existence of a few times and places where it is temporarily abandoned.

Politics and business are rarely discussed in mixed-sex company. These topics are, however, among the favorite topics of men when they are together in the absence of women. Undoubtedly there remains much of the traditional male attitude that attributed to women a lack of interest and aptitude for matters political and economic. The employment of many local women, at one time or another, in factories and textile mills has not sufficed to radically alter either the attitude or its behavioral consequences. One of the "withdrawal" tactics often employed by men to avoid "talkin' politics" in the presence of women is the silence that falls over a group of men engaged in political discussion whenever a woman appears on the scene. This occurs quite remarkably in stores or near election polling places; a woman entering the store brings almost total silence if the men's conversation has been about topics deemed inappropriate for women to hear, including politics, the telling of off-color stories, or the use of profanity. If the men find it necessary to discuss these subjects at one another's homes, the most frequently used ploy is for one to drive up to the other's house, honk the horn or call out to him, and then carry on their conversation in the confines of a parked car. Standing in the yard, if the visitor is afoot, is also an effective means of staying out of the earshot of women. Discussions among women are concerned, for the most part, with domestic and child-rearing activities. Some topics, such as the exchange of favorite recipes, are regarded as uninteresting to men. Other subjects, particularly those having to do with sex, are considered unfit for male ears.

Relationships between unrelated or distantly related men and women easily fall under suspicion of sexual misbehavior. Purely business relations, such as sharing a ride to a town or mill where both are employed, are usually not suspect. So, too, the kind of relations associated with being a coworker, as among men and women teaching in the Little Laurel school, are considered legitimate and respectable, although the limits to the personal element in these relations are very narrow. Friendship between males and females from puberty to old age is invariably assumed to include a strong sexual element. Platonic bonds between men and woman are simply not possible. Sometimes this extends outside the range of persons who might be sexually attracted to each other. A seventy-year-old woman, an informant whom I visited once or twice each week for over a year, would never invite me inside her home unless adult male kinsmen were present. It was appropriate, it seemed, for us to converse on her porch in full view of passing traffic, but the difference of forty years in our ages still did not allow more private association. The prohibition of this sort of encounter with younger women, of course, is more strictly observed. In sum, men's interest in women, and women's interest in men, is assumed to be sexual unless there are "good reasons" to believe otherwise. Good reasons include close kin ties where sexual interest would verge on incest, extreme age differences, and legitimate practical reasons for association. Companionship for the mere pleasure of being in each other's company is excluded.

THE TIES THAT BIND

Mother-in-law jokes are not amusing to people in the Little Laurel. This staple of urban conversation does not strike even the most urban-oriented individuals as a proper subject for joking. Each nuclear family in the Little Laurel, with few exceptions, has frequent contact with the nuclear families of each spouse. It is to the interest—economically, socially, and emotionally—of those involved in these numerous kin relationships to maintain them as harmoniously as possible. Hostility cannot be openly expressed between individual kinsmen without bringing in the loyalties that are expected to, and do in general, exist among kin. The isolation of the nuclear family, common to many urban situations, tends to make spouses and their children more dependent upon one another. Where, as in the Little Laurel, there are multiple linkages that bind each nuclear family to a number of kinsmen, and these bonds are reaffirmed by economic cooperation, social interaction, and so on, there is a tendency for the nuclear family to be less self-centered. A husband or wife in the Little Laurel is not so entirely dependent upon a spouse as are individuals in urban families. What Max Gluckman delineates for Africa is an apt summary of the situation in this valley:

> The general effect of this sort of kinship situation seems to be a dispersal of attachments, which may well be reflected in the relationship of spouses, so that emotional bonds in marriage do not outweigh other ties. There is a marked conventional division of labour between men and women, and the society disbelieves in platonic relationships between them. Men work and spend their leisure time with men, women with women (Gluckman 1956:77–78).

The tension surrounding the maintenance of friendly relationships with as many kinsmen as possible provides spouses with a delicate task of diplomatic balance. To obtain and keep the approval of one's kinsmen means that one must attempt to carry out one's fair share of kinship obligations. A Little Laurel woman, whose husband held a managerial job in a nearby textile mill and who was, like her husband, relatively urbanized in her attitudes, spoke to me repeatedly of her conflict of feelings about her husband's mother. Her husband's brother and sister, expected to bear equal shares of the burden of caring for the invalid mother, had not, according to this informant, carried out their obligation. This woman wanted to put her mother-in-law in a "rest home," and apportion the cost among the adult children, but felt uneasy about the gossip that could be expected to follow such a course of action. Neither in this case, nor in several other similar ones, was there any expression of ridicule or animosity for the mother-in-law. Indeed, the word is almost never used in the Little Laurel: men and women refer to her as "my wife's mother" or "my husband's mother." Keeping peace in the family appears to include, as a customary tactic, the consideration of parents of each spouse as having equal claims to aid and affection.

The deep personal involvement with kinsmen, and the strong sentiment it entails, has been widely observed in Southern Appalachia. Although it is usually treated sympathetically by social scientists, it strikes a few as an unfortunate anomaly, so thoroughly do they regard the urban, nuclear family as the American norm. A sociologist, for example, recently wrote about Southern Appalachia:

> Some young people simply never establish themselves as separate individuals. Nor are they encouraged to do so by their parents. Both parents and children maintain what may be termed a *clinging behavior* which may be based less upon genuine affection and shared activities than upon neurotic emotional entanglements characterized by a mutual resentment. Grown offspring who hate their parents cannot bear to be away from them. Migrants who have finally broken away suddenly and curiously return home at the slightest misfortunes (Ball 1971:75).

Only if measured by the standard of the perhaps imaginary American urban family, a nuclear family severed from other kinsmen and depending on a very small number of individuals for its emotional and social resources, does the Appalachian kinship group take on the color of abnormality. For most societies in the world, it is clearly unexceptional and represents a quite effective adaptation to the circumstances of isolation, extreme rurality, and self-sufficiency that characterized the region before 1940. That it now appears dysfunctional is due to the persistence of traditional beliefs and behavior into an era of change of drastic proportions.

5 / Land as place and property

As a geographical setting the valley forms a framework for local life and provides an historical anchor that reaches several generations into the past. One hears many tales studded with references to local geographical features and ancestors of residents. Stories of violence and supernatural intervention, of suspected adultery and calculated murder, are matter-of-factly tied to the Little Laurel by mention of the exact spot—"not twenty foot from Herman Banks' house"—where each event occurred. As signposts for giving directions, and as markers of historical events, local conversation bristles with references to outcroppings of rock, intermittent streams, long-erased roadbeds, and cornfields long overgrown with poplar trees. Walking across a hayfield one afternoon, my elderly companion stopped and said, entirely out of context with our discussion of local political intrigues, "Right here is where the old highway looped around, right here and then down to that old apple tree yonder." It had been forty years since the roadbed had changed, but its previous path still assumed importance. In like manner, the widespread and detailed knowledge of apt locations for abundant huckleberries, thick patches of galax, or bear haunts is part of daily life.

With a greater dependence on industrial jobs and widening contacts outside the valley, the importance of the valley itself, of land as place, gradually dims. Land has, to many residents, become more significant as property, and a careful eye is cast upon it as a financial investment. Land in the Little Laurel is shifting, in the view of its owners, from place to property. It is even now, however, rarely seen as solely one or the other, but as various and often ambiguously expressed mixtures of the two.

WHO OWNS THE LAND?

Most of the township of Little Laurel falls entirely within the boundaries of a national forest. Federally owned forest takes up over half the land area of the township. Taxable, privately owned land accounts for 17,331 acres. This is divided into 577 parcels of land, each separately listed on the county tax rolls. Very few of these tracts are listed under the same name, and few exceed 50 acres, although one local resident owns a total of 400 acres (Table 3).

TABLE 3   LAND OWNERSHIP IN THE LITTLE LAUREL, 1966*

Owner	Characteristics of Ownership					
	Number of Owners	Number of Acres	Percent of Total Acres	Average Size Holding	Largest Holding	Smallest Holding
Local[1]	364	8254	47.6	22.68	401	.25
Summer/ Retired[2]	119	2023	11.7	17.00	149	.125
Corporate[3]	8	2991	17.3	383.88	1115	10.00
Migrant Kin[4]	82	3306	19.1	40.32	350	0.5
Other[5]	4	757	4.4	189.25	573	20.0
Totals	577	17331	100.1	—	—	—

* Compiled by author from figures in Little Laurel tax lister's book.
[1] This includes those who have been resident in the valley for over twenty years. [2] Although some of these plots have no houses on them, the land was bought in order, it seems, to build summer or retirement homes. All plots in this category are small. [3] Included here is a nonprofit corporation that holds land to provide homes for the members of a cooperative "community" in the valley—it is the largest corporate holder. Others in this category are mining and land speculation companies. [4] In this category are those who have moved from the valley yet continue to own land there; in each case they are kinsmen of valley residents. [5] The largest plot in this category is owned by a wealthy man who has retired, and bought tracts of land throughout the county, but who does not reside in the Little Laurel.

To a remarkable extent, local residents and their kinsmen who have left the valley have retained title to the land in the valley. Land ownership is widespread, and the average size of holdings is quite small, just under 23 acres. If we combine out-migrating kinsmen with those who remain, we find that two-thirds of the valley's taxable land remains in their hands. Corporations have been slow to purchase land here, unlike the situation in many parts of Appalachia. Most of the land formerly owned by business corporations, particularly the lumber companies that stripped the forests in the early part of this century, now belongs to the national forest. Relatively little, too, has been sold to the summer people as sites for vacation cabins or to retired couples who expect to spend the remainder of their lives in the valley. With the exception of two men who have purchased tracts of over 100 acres each, these individual outsiders buy parcels of 5 to 20 acres each. The two larger tracts are being divided to be resold, at large profits, to those who come later looking for plots suitable for summer cabins or year-round retirement homes.

Ownership of land provides a rough indication of the level of prosperity in the valley. For example, in a settlement called Stony Branch, the poorest section of the valley, few persons own land; most residents of Stony Branch rent their homes from local merchants. There is a ready and ever-increasing market for land, and prices asked and received have increased enormously in the years 1955 to 1966. An acre of hilly woodland that sold for $50 to $100 in 1955 could have easily been sold ten years later for $450 and more. One man who owned a vacant tract of 3 acres on the main highway set his price in 1965 at, in his words, "one for one," ($1000 per acre) and felt confident of receiving what he asked, even though the land was without a stream and contained only a few scrubby trees. People are nevertheless astonished at the rapid rise in land prices and each disclosure of the amount "some Floridy man" has paid for a dilapidated farm brings expressions of amazement. Stories of fortunes lost when cheap land was available in the past, and there was no money to purchase it, are commonplace. Such tales usually center on land that was bought by outsiders (the large tract held by the cooperative community is a favorite example) and is now closed off to use by local people.

A MORAL RIGHT TO LAND

Yet holding legal title to land, while it is important to the residents of the valley, is only part of their attachment to the Little Laurel. Far more significant, it appears, is their sense of the valley as a matrix for their lives. Despite their willingness to pay high prices for land, the summer people—or, as they are most often labeled, "Floridy people"—are resented. They fence off the land, and local residents no longer have access to it for hunting and gathering of wild berries. They build cabins in areas that have long been clear of homes, high on the shoulders of the mountains and even, in a few cases, atop the peaks themselves. Since the cabins will be occupied only during the warm summer months, they need not consider the discomforts of bitter winter winds or roads choked with snow and ice. To set their cabin so as to get an unobstructed view of the opposite mountain range is, from the point of view of a summer resident, quite sensible. But for local people, traditional ideas of land use, the long-held notions of what is and what is not appropriate in building sites and fencing off one's tract, remain strong.

The "Floridy people" are frequently criticized in local conversation for their practice of fencing and posting their land against trespassers. This violates the custom of allowing free passage throughout the valley, whether for hunting, picking wild berries, pulling galax, or just walking.

Timber is recognized as private property and one must buy trees before cutting them. Scavenging for fallen tree limbs to use as firewood, however, falls into the same category as galax: it belongs to the gatherer. The same is true for wild fruits—huckleberries, blueberries, blackberries, and so on. For mineral rights, a landowner customarily received one-seventh or one-eighth of the proceeds from mining, an agreement that was more often written and notarized than were timber contracts.

The permanent residents do not dispute the legal right of a landowner to do as he will with his land, but the break in traditional patterns of free access to land is irritating. At dusk one summer evening, as lights began to appear in the windows of summer cabins high on the surrounding hillsides, one man tried to explain to me his own feelings:

Use to be, you could walk up there on Big Ridge from one end to the other and not see mor'n two or three houses. Hell, you can't walk or rabbit-hunt up there no more. These Floridy people come in here and buy a little patch of land and stick no trespassing signs all over it. This country [valley] used to belong to ever'body. Why, a man didn't care [didn't mind] at all to have people walking through his woods and hunting on his land. That just ain't the way it is, no more, though. If I had any land left, and wanted to sell to them summer people, I'd shore make 'em pay for the privilege of fencin' it off and puttin' up them signs. I'd make 'em pay a lot.

As has been remarked of other parts of Southern Appalachia, however, legal ownership of land confers almost unlimited rights. If one owns land abutting a creek, for example, he feels quite justified in using the creek banks and the stream itself to dispose of trash and sewage. Incidents of local men challenging government officials by daring them to "come on my place," and brandishing a shotgun or rifle to back up the dare, are numerous and are always recollected with wry admiration. When on one occasion I witnessed a drunken man become a nuisance in a local store, in a scene that has been repeated many times, he was dragged under protest into the highway, fortunately empty of traffic, with the declaration: "Now you're on land that's part your'n—don't come back on mine till you can act right." Quite similar sentiments apply to federally owned land that forms part of the national forest. Arrested for cutting a Christmas tree on national forest land, one man defended himself in federal court with this remark: "I was just getting a little bit of my part of them woods, judge." The requirement that those who collect evergreens from the national forest pay a nominal fee for a collecting permit is widely ignored with impunity. The practice, indeed, is so widespread that a person who bothers to secure a permit is the exception. Evergreen collectors take it as a game to evade the forest rangers and federal officers, and they declare that the officials have a similar playful attitude. As one elderly woman said as she sat at night tying the day's galax harvest into carefully counted bundles:

The way I look at hit, the good Lord put this land here for all of us to use and ain't nobody got no right to fence it off and try to tell people they can't pull galax on hit nowheres. It looks like they want to put a tax on just about anything you want to do; why, anymore, they won't even let a young'un fish less he's got a license.

THIS COUNTRY AND THIS PLACE

In local parlance, "this country" is used to refer to the Little Laurel, and, less frequently, to the valley and areas immediately adjacent to it. When one wants to indicate a wider expanse, usually restricted to the several connected counties in this part of the state, he says "this *whole* country." The geographical extent intended is clearly understood from the context. Such expressions as "Frank Bowditch's boundary [tract of land] is the biggest in this country," indicate that the speaker means the Little Laurel, while "There's nobody in this whole country that's as good at teachin' dogs as he is," just as surely means the area of several counties. The frequency with which people use "country" demonstrates, in a subtle but telling fashion, their sense of the Little Laurel and the surrounding areas as separate and distinctive. It is, from this point of view, a different kind of place, a "country" with its own historical traditions and customs.

"Place," too, is a word heard frequently in the valley. It is used to label a particular area and most often carries a connotation of ownership. If one, for example, wants to point out an individual's ownership of a tract of unoccupied pasture or woodland, the preferred term is "boundary." Where one lives, the land and outbuildings surrounding his residence, is called his "place," and the same term is used for buildings used for carrying on one's occupation. A store, for example, is sometimes referred to as "Bob Wilson's place," but more commonly as "Bob Wilson's." Wilson's residence, particularly if it includes more than a residence—that is, if it resembles a traditional farm layout—will be called "Wilson's place."

When one says, as a middle-aged man did to me one day in explaining his return to the valley after decades of "following construction" work, "My place is here; I belong here," the meaning was ambiguous only in that it was unclear if he owned land or not. There was no uncertainty that he intended two separate things: that his childhood had been spent here and that he felt himself at ease in the valley.

A number of terms are used to pinpoint locations. "Up the river" is perhaps the most common, meaning upstream, and this is usually applied to directions on the highway that parallels the river through the valley; "up the highway" or "up the road" points to the same direction as "up the river." "Across the mountain" is another commonly used term, and usually indicates a location on the farther side of Big Ridge, while "down the mountain" indicates the area on the far side—or "yon side" in local terms—of the Sourwood Mountains. "Across the river" is a phrase used to indicate the less densely settled area east of the Little Laurel River. In addition to these orienting terms, there are a number of others used, particularly in roughly dividing the creeks into residential areas. Wildcat Creek is thickly settled, and is divided in local parlance into "Upper" and "Lower" Wildcat. Other streams and ridges are treated in the same way.

Specific descriptive terms are often used. A "flat" refers to a level tract of ground, as in the expression "He lives in that first flat down the mountain." And, in similar concrete fashion, a "straight" is used to refer to stretches of highway that contain few bends and turns.

The idea, expressed in a variety of ways, that people who have been reared in the Little Laurel, and more generally in this section of the Southern Appalachians, firmly belong here is unanimous. The only reason for one to leave the valley is for the better economic opportunities afforded elsewhere. No one, it is almost universally believed, leaves the Little Laurel because he prefers the style of life elsewhere. "We ole hillbillies just don't fit in nowhere else but here in these mountains," was one expression given me on this topic, and the same meaning was conveyed constantly in a number of phrasings. In a rare moment of generalizing, a storekeeper remarked on the differences between mountain people and other Americans:

Northerners, most of 'em, are raised and educated in a way that makes them think nothing of moving around all over the country all the time—they just don't have any certain place that they call home. And they don't feel bashful in all that moving around, so they don't ever feel the need of a place to get back to. But these people in the mountains; they're all a poor class of people and they just don't know how to act when they get away from the mountains.

When explanations are offered for the return of migrants who had expressed an intention to leave the valley permanently, they are invariably cast in terms that have to do with the geographical peculiarity of the region. In a typical example, the return of James Marshall and his family was explained to me by his brother-in-law:

James went off out there to Washington [state] last year, and he said he's going to stay. I been out there—they's little towns no bigger'n Chesterville, and it's got mountains. Looks a lot like here. But James is just like me, I reckon, cause he got to missin' these mountains. They's just something about being here all your life that gets in your blood, I guess. They's no way in this world you don't miss it, and I mean hard, too. So he's just like everybody else—they go off, but they always come back, somehow.

Another man, with years of experience of working in factories in California, Michigan, and Ohio, was asked if he had ever thought of staying away from the Little Laurel. "Oh, yes," he replied, "I took a notion one time to just live out there in Californy till I died. But, you know, I couldn't. It just got so it'd make me sick to think about these mountains back here. I had to come back to this country."

Even when they don't return to live in the valley, migrants make frequent visits to their birthplace. Weekend traffic from the Washington–Baltimore area and from cities in Ohio and Pennsylvania crowds the highways throughout Southern Appalachia, and the Little Laurel receives its share of these migrants who return home for a few hours on one or two weekends every month. Trips of twelve or fourteen hours are made almost nonstop, with only quick pauses at service stations and roadside coffee shops. Between trips, and particularly for those migrants who live too far (for example, Boston, Denver, the West Coast), long-distance telephone calls keep kinsmen in weekly or more frequent contact. Letter writing between kinsmen is relatively rare, even among those who have completed high school, and direct contact, either by telephone or weekend visiting, is preferable.

There are some families in the Little Laurel who have become seasonal migrants, spending half a year in the valley, usually during the winter months, and living elsewhere for the remaining half-year. According to the elementary school principal, each November sees thirty to forty children arriving to enroll in the Little Laurel School. Then, before the school year is complete, they leave with their parents for Oregon, Michigan, or other areas where jobs are obtainable and wages are high. Certainly the local dictum that everybody who leaves always comes back is not true in any literal sense, but as an expression of desire, perhaps, there is some significance to it. Few people seem to leave for permanent residence elsewhere without expressions of regret and promises to return for frequent visits. In summer many who now make their homes in the suburbs of Detroit or

Chicago return with their families to take their annual vacation with kinsmen in the valley.

In stark contrast with the usual pattern of frequent communication and visiting was the case of a man who, having left the Little Laurel "for the West" in 1905, was not heard from again until 1967. So astounded was the man's younger brother at receiving a letter from him after sixty years of silence that he at first found it almost impossible to believe that the brother still lived. The news of the receipt of the letter spread rapidly up and down the valley, and for weeks it was a prime topic of conversation. Two elderly men recalled how they had driven the man 30 miles across the Sourwood Mountains in 1905 to the nearest railroad depot. His failure to communicate with his family was blamed, with great assurance, on his marriage to a Californian; her death and the prospects of spending his last years alone, said the letter, occasioned his belated attempt to reestablish ties with his relatives. Within a few weeks his youngest sister was dispatched to California to make certain that he was not in need, and there were plans for his return to the Little Laurel. This particular case was cited to me repeatedly as one of the very few instances of someone having left the Little Laurel and not returning. "Nearly everybody here goes away some time or other, but they always come back, sometime, somehow," commented one man. "I guess sixty-two years is the record, but even ol' Sam Hall couldn't stand to die without seeing his folks again."

HISTORICAL TRADITIONS AND PLACE

Part of this sense of attachment can be seen in the numerous tales, based on historical events, one hears in the Little Laurel. In one of these, a man was killed during a turkey shoot in a village several miles from the valley. It was during the winter of 1888, and Tom Williams and Tull Henshaw, both from the Little Laurel, went to try their luck at winning the turkey (awarded for most accurately firing a rifle at a target). After Henshaw fired, he started to walk downrange to check his target, and Williams, at this point very drunk, called out that if he (Henshaw) went any further, he would shoot him. Henshaw continued to walk downrange and Williams shot and killed him. A few months later, Williams was tried, found guilty, and sentenced to be hung. When "hanging day" came in February, the weather was bitterly cold, with mixed snow and sleet almost obscuring vision, but the town was crowded with onlookers there to watch the spectacle. After that, miserably cold winter days were always said to be "as bad as the day Tom Williams was hung." Even now, among elderly men, the expression is occasionally heard and when it is, it usually provokes a retelling of the tale of Williams and Henshaw. Williams' descendants, among them three great-grandsons who are prosperous shrubbery dealers, still live in the valley, and speak of their great-grandfather's behavior, or at least the event itself, with undisguised pride in his notoriety. The exact location of the turkey shoot, and precisely where the gallows stood, can be pointed out by men today, and figure prominently in the telling of the event. That is, it seems important that the storyteller pause at certain times to point out that "they're shooting right east—not more'n thirty yards—of where that new pants factory is built."

Another often-heard story concerns a woman's murder by her husband, who almost escaped. Raymond Robinson, sometime in the 1890s, had killed his wife and reported that she had died in her sleep. Living well back in the woods, he was able to build a coffin and put her corpse in it without being observed. Then, as the coffin was riding to the family cemetery on a wagon, the funeral cortege was halted by the sudden appearance of the county "high sheriff," who had been notified that murder had been committed and insisted on examining the body. "Why, it was right there by Herman Banks' house where they took out the body, and laid it on a quilt," was the way one man related the exact place where the procession stopped. "Right there by that big chestnut oak in Herman's yard," it was discovered that the woman's neck and back were broken. Her husband was immediately arrested and charged with murder.

There is some disagreement about how the sheriff's suspicions were aroused. When the tale is told by elderly men, it is said that the murdered woman's brother, who lived "across the mountain" in another county, had dreamed of her death during the night and, on the strength of his dream, went to the sheriff. Younger men, in discussing this aspect of the tale, agree that it has always been said to be due to the dream that Robinson was captured, but they are not convinced by the "supernatural" element. As a forty-year-old man conjectured, "You know, Robinson probaly came home that night and caught some man with his wife. He got out the window, saw Robinson kill her, then rode his horse over that mountain to tell about it. Then her brother just said he dreamed it to cover up what she'd been doing." This man thinks that, like all tales, this one "just got bigger in the telling," although neither he nor anyone else disagrees with the factual points in the story. And, to old and young alike, the geographical features are definite and important—not only the location of the examination of the corpse, but the distance from the murderer's house across the mountain to the man who said he dreamed it. Their intimate knowledge of the terrain enables them to provide plausible alternatives to the dream.

Another tale, of the "escaped lawbreaker," provides an example of a theme common to discussion of people leaving the valley for other parts of the United States. About 1910, goes the story as told by a seventy-year-old man,

John Boone and a feller from out at Hoot Owl had ordered their Christmas whiskey, and they had to go over here to Bragtown to get it at the [railroad] depot. Well, they rode over there and back on mules, and put a gallon jug in each end of a poke [cloth sack] and slung it across their mules in front of them. When they got down here to where the road makes that sharp turn at Walt Silver's house, they met some ole boys who's drinkin' and stumblin' along. Wayne Smith and Charlie McIntosh was with them, and Charlie—he's drunk as a dog anyhow—asked John if he could have a drink of that likker he got at the depot. John told him he couldn't get to it right then, to come on up to the house and they'd both drink some of it. They rode on down the road a piece, and Charlie took out his pistol, turned back, and shot at John. Well, them ole drunk boys went on around the turn in the road before they knowed what happened, and Wayne says to Charlie, "Put that damned gun away, you fool, you're liable to kill somebody." I tell you, he already had killed John Boone. He fell right off that mule and died right there in front of Walt Silver's house. The law come down here and got Charlie, and the first trial up in Chesterville gave him hanging. He got another lawyer and they had another trial, over in Bragtown, and the judge give Charlie seventeen years in the state prison. After twelve years, he escaped and lit out for Kansas and never did come back to this country. I heard he married out there and started him another family.

THE OLD HOME PLACE

It is considered desirable to retain ownership in the land one was reared on and, if practicable, to keep possession of the childhood home of one's parents. Many people live in houses built sixty years and more ago by their parents and inherited upon their parents' death. One man, a bachelor, lives in the small cabin built by his grandfather as a log cabin—a "pole house"—that has since been covered in "brick siding," an asphalt covering marked to resemble brick. Although it is exceptional for one house to remain this long in the possession of the same family, the sentiment for keeping title to the family land and houses is strong. Upon inheritance, some tracts of land are owned by large numbers of people and, lacking agreement on the disposition of the property, it remains intact regardless of sentiment. Low real estate taxes make this situation relatively painless from an economic point of view. Meanwhile, the land steadily increases in value and can be regarded as a solid financial investment if one is not meticulous about "keeping the old home place."

This man, almost 75 years old, was born and has lived all his life in this house, a log cabin now covered with imitation brick siding. In the background, a shed built more recently than the house is covered with hand-made shakes.

Some people, however, have convinced themselves that, whatever profit can be made by selling the "old home place," they have a moral obligation to keep it intact for their heirs. Few of these houses are lived in, and some sit in the middle of heavy woods, gradually and peacefully decomposing.

More frequently, one encounters individuals who have, after years of bargaining or slow accumulation of savings, managed to buy the house they lived in as children. It is then remodeled with a bathroom and kitchen. One of the "summer people," a man whose ancestors settled in a log cabin in the Kentucky mountains, has transported his father's cabin, log by log, to a hillside in the Little Laurel. It has been reassembled and modern insulation and plumbing added to make a snug year-round vacation house for the family. Since this man's wife lived as a child only 10 miles from the Little Laurel, the compromise—his father's house near her family's land—is satisfactory to both. In another case, the ancestral pole house sits in the midst of a large dairy pasture and is used for storage of hay and farm tools.

As urban influence crept into the valley, pole houses began to stand out as reminders of an impoverished and "backwoodsy" past. In many cases, the hewn logs of these houses received a sheathing of planks and were transformed into ordinary frame structures. In the past decade, however, as people here have become aware of the desire of tourists to buy and rent "authentic" log cabins, the sheathing has been ripped away to reveal the rustic logs beneath. One prosperous man has begun scouting the Southern Appalachians for log cabins, which he buys and transports to his property in the valley and has reassembled. "McIntyre's

A fine example of nineteenth-century architecture in the Little Laurel, this house sits in a cow pasture and is used for storing hay and tools.

Purchased in Kentucky, this house was taken apart, the logs carefully numbered, and is now being set on a new foundation in the Little Laurel. It will be sold as a summer cabin.

Rhododendron Park," as his vacation-housing development is known, contained six of these reconstructed cabins in 1966, with more due to arrive from Kentucky and Tennessee. In such cases as this, the monetary worth of nostalgia and authenticity, however contrived, has been well recognized.

The firm cement of place and history is rapidly loosening, as log cabins are taken apart and put together again like children's toys, as land is sold to outsiders, and perhaps most significantly, as land takes on the qualities of property rather than place. The attitude is rarely expressed in an unambiguous manner. Views of the valley and one's stake in its land vary from one individual to another. Mack Higgins, for example, a man of wide occupational experience in the world outside the Little Laurel, said that a "Floridy man" had offered a good price for part of his forty-five acre farm, but he would not sell, since "it just don't seem right to break up a good farm like that." His traditional ideas and his unequivocal view of the land are shared by few in the Little Laurel. The opinion of a storekeeper, in considering the potential of the valley, is more frequently encountered. As he looked off to the peaks of the Craggies, he said, "Our mountains are just being ruined. And we let 'em do it." Less than ten minutes later, he was enthusiastically discussing his plans to build and operate a motel and campground.

His attitude, a vague, disturbed sense of loss combined with an eagerness to exploit the financial possibilities of the land, is quite widely held.

Meanwhile, the flood of summer visitors to the valley, both those who vacation in their own cabins and those who pitch their tents in the national forest campgrounds, rises each year. Forest rangers recorded over 30,000 campers in a single campground in the summer of 1967. The total for the valley, including the three private campgrounds operated by local residents, easily exceeded 60,000. It is a deluge that local people cannot long resist, and there are many signs that the entrepreneurial opportunities are being grasped. One local stockeeper, in the summer of 1966, began renting small motorcycles to tourists and local boys. Another converted a log cabin into a gift shop and rented it.

During the summer months, the valley takes on an aura of businesslike bustle that is sharply different from wintertime. Tourists and summer people shop in local stores, and their cars pass up and down the highway. The local custom of waving to every passing automobile, pronounced in the quieter months of winter, is

Looking across the valley, toward the Craggy Mountains. Although heavy snow rarely isolates the valley for more than a few hours, the tempo of life in wintertime is considerably slower than that of the summer.

abandoned in the busy traffic of summer, when one waves only at those he can easily identify. As the tourists depart, and life slows to a winter tempo, strange autos are given close examination. There remains, despite the growing numbers of summer visitors and the easier accessibility of the world outside the Little Laurel, a sense that only those who belong in the valley, who have been reared here, will be seen in the Little Laurel during the winter. It is a time when local people return to rhythms of life more like those of previous years. Even so, most residents are only indirectly concerned with tourists, as they watch the flow of traffic on the highway or give directions to inquiring passersby. Snowfalls, never heavy or long-standing, do not isolate them as they once did, when snowplows were unknown and travel was slow and laborious. Yet the absence of summertime vacationers brings a quietness to the valley that excludes, subtly but surely, the intrusions of the world outside.

6 / Settlement and community

People in the Little Laurel are bound together by common interests and share a sense of unity. They are thus easily considered a community in the usual sociological sense. Within the valley, a number of distinctions, sometimes overlapping and rarely exclusive, are made, primarily among ten named neighborhoods or "settlements," as they are known here. Names for these residential areas range from geographic features (Big Ridge, Wildcat Creek) to man-made features (Wilson's Chapel, Soapstone Road) to family names (Tolson, Grierson's Holler). Other locales receive occasional recognition. When giving directions, for example, people are likely to mention such places as "Upper Street," meaning an area of twenty-odd houses strung along a high-winding road. There is, in this case, an acknowledged irony in the name, since many residents of Upper Street are poor and Saturday night drunkenness and brawling are frequent there.

Only when there is an intervening unpopulated area, as in the separation of Big Ridge from other settlements, are boundaries clearly defined. But more than geography sets off the settlements; they are distinguished as well by association with particular family names, occupational specialties, moral reputation, and the existence of separate institutions. Each of these factors merits consideration.

FAMILY NAMES

Where a newly married couple resides is said to be a matter of their choice, but there are limitations. A man's family, if they own sufficient land, will offer him a homesite near his parents. This will later be deducted from his part of the inheritance. If for some reason his family does not provide a new home, the wife's kinsmen will usually make the offer. It is not often that newlyweds rent. The result of this practice of settling near parents is to cluster related persons in separate settlements. Over time this has included the naming of cemeteries after families; one finds a "Higgins Cemetery" in one settlement, a "Hall Cemetery" in another. In recent years, the graves are not always of those related to these families, but there remains a strong tendency to bury kinsmen where there is a known kin link with those who lie beside them.

Settlements are made up, in most cases, of several "sets" of kinsmen. Big Ridge contains households of Halls, Higginses, Wilsons, Henshaws, and

McIntoshes. Halls and Henshaws also live in Tolson. Other settlements follow a similar pattern. Thus any single settlement contains more than one kin-related group and each kin group is spread out into more than one settlement. Just as one commonly follows the political and religious affiliation of his parents, so does he live near either his own or his spouse's parents. Exceptions are cited, as in matters of kinship obligation, as needing explanation: "Hester told Bud when they married that she wouldn't live with his people and he wouldn't live with her'n—so they went off down here to Tolson and built a house."

OCCUPATIONAL SPECIALTY

Until about thirty years ago, there was a rather close fit between a family's settlement and the occupation of the heads of household, so that, for instance, men who "followed the trade" of mica mining tended to live in the Soapstone Road settlement, and those who logged for their living built their homes nearer the heavily forested southern end of the valley, in Tolson or Grierson's Holler. The growth of industrial employment, the buying and selling of land rather than merely inheriting it, and the influx of outsiders has blurred this pattern. Nevertheless, in 1967 it was still discernible. No man engaged in logging lived in the Soapstone area, and those who bought and sold shrubbery were disproportionately represented in Big Ridge. Thirty years ago, when travel was by foot or horse and wagon, there was a practical reason for this occupational-residential segregation. With the advent of access to automobiles, however, the cogent reasons to live close by the site of one's work rapidly disappeared. In parallel fashion, changes occur in the tendency to reside in one's parental settlement. The ease with which a young wife can drive to visit her parents erases the former urgency for living within an hour's walk from her "people." Considerations of family sentiment, financial situation and changes in land ownership now play larger roles than occupation in the selection of residence.

MORAL REPUTATION

Reputation is another guideline people use to mark off areas. The poorest area in the valley, relatively isolated at the head of Stony Branch and accessible only by a winding dirt road, is said to be a dangerous neighborhood. Saturday nights in Stony Branch, people say, are "the most un-Christian thing around here." People in Stony Branch are the poorest, most ill-educated and ill-housed, and most "backwoodsy" (a term of derision) in the entire Little Laurel, according to those who live elsewhere. The residents themselves have quite different opinions, and they blame the trash-littered roadsides and Saturday drunkenness on people from other parts of the valley. As one Stony Branch woman said: "Hit's not the people down in here that do all the drinking they're blamed for—people come in here on Saturday night from all over. It hain't the people in here. People talk about how hit's such a bad place down in here, but that jest ain't true. There're good people down here." Their reputation, whether deserved or not, is probably related to the short period of time most Stony Branch families have been in the Little Laurel. Most residents have moved in within the past thirty years.

By rather sharp contrast, Rampton, a settlement lying along the main highway at the opposite end of the valley, enjoys a reputation as highly respectable and affluent. It is conspicuously represented by several brick and substantial frame houses along the main road, and contains relatively few very poor households. Two brick churches, Baptist and Methodist, stand together at Rampton's main crossroads, and two stores, one of them the largest and most profitable in the valley, face each other across the highway. For many decades, Rampton has been generally regarded as the most sophisticated neighborhood and, in the 1920s, it was only here that one could find automobiles and telephones. Several informants pointed out to me that the frequent news stories on poverty in Appalachia failed to tell the whole story by ignoring the existence of such settlements as Rampton.

As in most things, there is significant change in settlement reputation. Over the past twenty years, Big Ridge, formerly isolated up on the mountain spur from which it takes its name, has become known as a "progessive"—that is, urban-oriented—area. Even so, in 1967 it was still tinged with a reputation of backwardness dating from the time when it was connected to other settlements by a twisting dirt road. People in Big Ridge were the last in the Little Laurel to use the crude horse-drawn sleds once widely seen throughout the steeper parts of the valley. After about 1953, when the road up the mountain to it was paved, Big Ridge underwent rapid change and, a decade later, had four new brick homes with lawns and play yards quite like those of any American suburb.

BLURRING THE SEPARATIONS

For many decades there have been some factors that blurred the lines of distinction among these settlements. Until 1952, there were five two-room schoolhouses scattered throughout the valley. Children walked to the nearest school, and parents contributed time and effort to repair the school building, much as they do now for church buildings. Some schools served a single settlement. In most, however, children from several settlements came together. For teachers involved in these small schools there was an implicit ranking of teaching posts. It was widely known that a job in the Rampton school was preferable to one at Grierson's Holler. To be assigned to teach at Big Ridge was to be banished, and chances for promotion were correspondingly lower for teachers in these less desirable positions.

Political subdivisions, too, tended to bring together people from different settlements. Only after World War II was the entire valley redrawn into a single political township. Until then there were five separate townships in the Little Laurel, each with its own school and appointed officials.

The last small post office disappeared from the valley in 1965, but there had been a long period of gradual centralization in postal service and, one by one, the postal stations closed. Picking up the mail at these small rural stations allowed for daily visiting and gossiping with neighbors. They were housed in a convenient store and the storekeeper would frequently read aloud the letters received by his illiterate customers. News from those who had left the valley was thus provided for larger numbers of people than a single household. Since the 1960s mail has been delivered directly to each house by carrier from the main post office in the county seat. Letters are now read at home, and post offices, formerly a focal point for settlements and combinations of settlements, are extinct.

Church congregations are not drawn from single settlements. Even when a church of one's own denomination exists near home, one might attend a similar church in another settlement. In any congregation families from several settlements will be represented. Speaking for what he saw as "progress," a fifth-grade teacher in the consolidated elementary school told me that churches should go the way of schools, that it was a waste of money and energy to maintain a number of separate churches. Joined together, he said, "each large church could afford a nice building and a full-time preacher. Every one of them could hold regular services on Sunday." His view that the main impediment was the objection of the various ministers was not borne out by other informants. There seemed to be little sentiment in the Little Laurel for abandoning even the smallest and most poorly financed church. Sharing ministers and jointly sponsoring various activities have been the means of maintaining distinct churches on restricted budgets.

As a single church is attended by people from a number of settlements, the customers of any store in the valley are also representative of different areas. People do not often confine their purchases to only one store. They are likely to trade with a storekeeper who is a kinsman or friend, unless he is at an inconvenient distance. Poorer families, who lack automobiles and must buy on credit, are more

Like many churches in the region, the Wildcat Creek Baptist Church, shown here, must share a minister with one or more other churches. Repair and maintenance on the building and its grounds are done by the volunteer labor of its members.

In some parts of the Little Laurel, people must still cross footbridges to reach their homes. The state highway department has installed several suspension bridges (top), but a few people still rely on bridges made from scraps of lumber and wire. (bottom).

restricted in their choice of store or church. They buy from stores nearest their homes, and from storekeepers who will grant them credit. Since, as we shall see in a later chapter, stores are not only places where goods are bought, but are also centers for the dissemination of information, there is a remarkable amount of shopping (and gossiping) by any one family in a number of different stores.

FROM SETTLEMENT TO COMMUNITY

The process of consolidation of the valley, in economic dependency or in community sentiment, has not occurred overnight. Settlements are not likely to disappear as distinctive sections of the valley for some time. Yet when Little Laurel School opened in 1952, including all neighborhoods by 1953, change was, according to those who taught there, rapid and thoroughgoing. Children from Big Ridge joined the school in 1953, after the road to the top of the mountain was paved and regarded as safe for school buses. Big Ridge pupils, as the teachers recall, were very "bashful and clannish"; other children saw them as "hickey or backwoodsy." This was not simply a reflection of economic differences; Big Ridge people lived as well as others in the Little Laurel. But the life style of people from this formerly isolated area was more rural and inward-looking. Bib overalls for boys and barefoot for boys and girls was the dress for children from "up on the mountain." When they first attended the consolidated school, they wore the same. Within less than half a year, however, their dress conformed to that of other settlements. Yet Big Ridge in the late 1960s was still viewed as set apart from other parts of the valley.

Easier transportation has been a chief factor in breaking down neighborhood distinctiveness in the Little Laurel. As people turn to factory jobs, commuting daily or weekly from home to work and back again, they become less attuned to the minutiae of daily life in their own neighborhood. Seeing people from other parts of the valley more frequently, the commuter is more likely to consider them as potential neighbors, and can easily bring himself to move to another part of the valley. There are no longer the compelling reasons of a former era—proximity to parents, familiarity with a childhood home, and so forth—to spend a lifetime in one neighborhood. The sense of unity that, from the accounts of older residents, appears to have attached to people in a single neighborhood in an earlier time has been enlarged to include the entire valley. One man, reared in the Wildcat Creek neighborhood, spoke about his marriage forty years ago: "Why I didn't even know she was in the world. Never even heard tell of her people. But they'd been living up there on Big Ridge for longer than mine had been down here. People in them days just didn't get around the way they do now." Fifty years ago, it is fair to say, some neighborhoods of the Little Laurel were communities, relatively isolated and self-sufficient.

Ties of friendship, too, are more dispersed than formerly. Almost always, one's friends are those, very likely kinsmen, whom one has known and associated with since childhood. Friendship reaches across settlements and links people together. Again, rapid transportation aids short and frequent visits to areas that were once seen only on rare occasions; friends can be visited almost daily and on the spur of the moment. A number of my male informants would, in a single day, see their friends in four or five settlements. To remain in one's own settlement for an entire week is, in this modern era, considered excessively "clannish," even for very poor families.

There is a great deal of cooperation among religious groups, in spite of what, to an outsider, might seem excessive inefficiency and competitiveness in the desire to maintain a number of struggling but separate congregations. Two Baptist churches, the largest in the valley, share a minister. He preaches "morning service" at one church, eats Sunday dinner with a member-family on a rotating basis, then leads another service 3 miles down the valley at another Baptist church. A regular weekly evening of hymn singing brings together the Baptist congregations of two other churches in the spring and summer. Only the difficulty and uncertainty of wintertime travel prevents this from continuing throughout the year. The similarity of doctrine, implicitly recognized as the basis of cooperative "socials" among Baptists, Methodists, and Presbyterians—all founded on fundamentalist Protestant belief—is another means of diminishing the separateness of churches. By the early 1960s all major churches of any given denomination in the valley were using the same mass-produced literature for their Bible classes.

In summer, the largest churches hold daily "vacation Bible schools" for a period of ten days to two weeks. These sessions are scheduled so that no two schools operate during the same two weeks. Thus there is, each summer, a series of such daily Bible schools in the valley. A few mothers use them as child-care centers, sending children to one school after the other for much of the summer. Similar care is taken in setting times for "revivals," when ministers from outside the region preach in a single church nightly for a week or two: revivals in the valley are not held simultaneously.

Decoration Day (the high point of the year for churches) is an important religious ceremony in the valley. This is a designated Sunday in June or July when families gather to honor the dead by "decorating" graves, cleaning and trimming cemetery plots, and holding special church services. Decoration Day, having similar importance and calling forth similar activities as Memorial Day in other parts of the United States, is variable in scheduling. Since any individual (or his spouse) might have an obligation to celebrate the occasion in more than one cemetery, Decoration Days are set by a cooperative effort; no two burying grounds hold the ceremony on the same Sunday. Formerly, in some sections of Southern Appalachia, such annual activities were collective funeral ceremonies. Horace Kephart observed that in 1913:

> In all back settlements that I have visited, from Kentucky southward, there is a strange custom as to the funeral sermon, that seems to have no analogue elsewhere. It is not preached until long after the interment, maybe a year or several years. In some districts the practice is to hold joint services, at the same time and place, for all in the neighborhood who died within the year. The time chosen will be after the crops are gathered, so that everybody can attend. In other places a husband's funeral sermon is postponed until his wife dies, or *vice versa*, though the interval may be many years. These collective funeral services last two or three days, and are attended by hundreds of people, like a camp-meeting (Kephart 1922:335).

Informants in the Little Laurel recalled only that, in an earlier time, Decoration Day sermons served to memorialize all the dead for the previous year, but that funeral services were almost always held individually when burial occurred.

Membership and attendance in a particular church now depend far less upon residence near the church, or upon kinship ties, than was true only twenty-five or thirty years ago. There are four Baptist churches in the valley, but only one Methodist and one Presbyterian. Two others house small evangelical sects that are founded from time to time by the sudden inspiration of local part-time preachers. Few of these groups survive for more than five or ten years. Given the number and denominations of the churches, it is obvious that one's church membership will often be in a group outside one's settlement. Baptists, as is the case throughout Appalachia, greatly outnumber the members of other religious groups.

Politically, the distinctions of settlement remain only as an informal consideration in "getting out the vote" and insuring that delegates to the county convention are geographically representative of the valley as a whole. The Little Laurel is a single township. Balloting in elections is held at a single site, the consolidated elementary school, and party township meetings of Democrats and Republicans, called to select delegates to the county conventions, are held in the school auditorium. In making up slates of candidates for the position of delegate, and in assigning people to provide transportation to the polls, political leaders in the

Although most churches in the Little Laurel have an appearance of affluence, some, like the one shown here, are simply converted residences.

Little Laurel take care to see that all neighborhoods are represented. Finally, there is a single registrar of voters for the township, one person responsible for "listing" personal property for taxation, and a three-man "school committee" to manage the elementary school. These offices, all appointive, are filled by residents of the valley from a number of different neighborhoods. In their efforts to include the entire valley, the calculations of political leaders reflect the importance still attached to settlements. Voters, it is widely recognized, are far more likely to participate in elections if there are candidates from their own or adjacent selttements.

THE CONSOLIDATED SCHOOL

Within the valley, the consolidated school provides the single institutional setting for activities—political, educational, and ceremonial—that explicitly draw together residents from the entire community. Widespread interest in the operation of the school exists, not only because many families have children enrolled, but also due to the desirability of employment there. Relatively low-paying jobs such as school cafeteria worker, janitor, and school bus driver provide a degree of economic security, a regular paycheck, that is unusual in local society. A job as school-teacher, due to the relatively high income and prestige attached to the position, is especially sought after.

Traditionally, jobs in the school system, including teaching positions ,are used as political rewards for kinsmen and friends of workers in the Democratic party. In recent years, a few Republican teachers have been hired, but they find it convenient to play a minor role, if any, in party politics. The county school board is invariably made up of Democrats since its membership must be approved by the state legislature, a body firmly under Democratic control. There were, in 1966, four teachers (of a total of nine) who were Republican; in the words of the principal, "I wouldn't swear to it, but I think—I'm pretty sure—four of them are Republican." As a staunch Democrat, he finds it best to underplay the role of politics in school hiring policies, a matter of intense controversy. This was the highest percentage of Republican teachers in any of the county's schools, a consequence, in the principal's view, of the higher proportion of Republican voters in the Little Laurel than in other townships. But the fact that political preferences of all teachers are known indicates that politics is not an inconsequential matter for employees at the school.

Indeed politics, school employment, and kinship are closely bound together. The school principal provides an instructive case. His father taught in Kent County schools for seventeen years before he quit to become a rural mail carrier ("it just got on his nerves," says his son). Two of the principal's brothers teach in the elementary school of another township, and another brother is the high school athletics coach. One brother's wife (a daughter of the county school superintendent) and a sister also hold teaching positions in other county schools. And in 1966 the principal's wife was attending a nearby college with the expectation of obtaining a teaching job in the Little Laurel upon graduation. Rarely are teachers hired who do not have ties of kinship with those already employed in the school system.

Equally stringent are the requirements for school janitor and lunchroom worker. These jobs are controlled by the township school committee (three men in the Little Laurel) which consults with the local principal on who is to be hired. With the same regularity as for teachers, the positions are filled by loyal Democrats who are kinsemen of committee members, school board members, or other local political leaders.

School jobs, especially teaching positions, are by local standards very well paid. A single state-wide salary schedule prevails. Given the generally low income of Kent County people, this places teachers' pay well above the average income. Kent ranks eighty-fifth among the state's 100 counties in the proportion of families receiving less than $3000 per year. Only 9 percent of the county school funds are raised locally. An annual salary of $7000 to $10,000, the range for teachers, is substantially higher than most.

Not only for those families who have a financial or political interest in the activities of Little Laurel School, but for the entire valley community, the school serves as a ceremonial center. It is the scene of various nonacademic celebrations, the most important of which is perhaps the annual Halloween Carnival. Sponsored by the teaching staff, the Carnival, aside from its entertainment purposes, is used as a means of raising money to supplement the school budget. During the week preceding the Carnival, parents are asked to contribute refreshments and household articles to be auctioned off. Raffle tickets are sold, for such prizes as (in 1966) 40 gallons of fuel oil. Local storeowners give table lamps, skillets, and other items for the auction. Admission is charged (fifty cents for adults, twenty-five cents for children), a band provides music, and a costume contest is held for younger children (six to nine years old) Various booths are set up in the school cafeteria: cake walks, dart throws, haunted houses, and so on. Music from the band, made up of young men hired from Masonville, consists of loud drum and electric guitar renditions of popular tunes.

The high point of the evening is the auction. An auctioneer is selected beforehand by the school principal, and is usually a political leader. The post is especially desirable for an aspirant for county political office. Offering items for bid, the auctioneer singles out individuals and jokingly makes demands for them to bid: "Frank, here's what your wife's been after for a long time—it oughta be worth at least five dollars," for example, as he holds up an arrangement of plastic flowers. Whoever is called upon in this way is expected to make a bid or toss a wisecrack back at the auctioneer. Prominent members of the community are expected to make bids that are obviously far more than the market price of the items. The entire event is suffused with banter from the audience and the auctioneer, a constant joking commentary on the bidder, exaggerated remarks about the usefulness of the item for sale, and what influences the purchase. Women, who generally remain silent during these exchanges, obviously enjoy the proceedings and from time to time will encourage their husbands to make or raise bids. Throughout, the auctioneer reminds the audience that all proceeds go to the improvement of the school, and announces the name of the contributor of each item.

Collections for improvement of the school and donated labor on its buildings and grounds are almost constant. When, shortly after its opening in 1952, the new

Parent-Teacher Association decided to construct a gymnasium, volunteers for labor and donations of building materials were quickly heard from. In 1966 the school needed a new piano for its auditorium, and collection jars were set out on the counter of every store in the valley. Girl Scouts in the Little Laurel have learned, when asked by illiterate or ill-educated residents if their cookie sale is "for the school," that a positive answer will usually bring about a sale.

Whether the topic is employment possibilities, county politics, or the changing economy, the Little Laurel School is a central issue. It has become a symbol of the valley as a community, just as its physical plant has taken on the role of ceremonial center for social and political activities.

STATUS AND PRESTIGE

In any public gathering, but most notably those which occur at the school, there is a pervasive air of informality in dress and behavior that closely reflects the opinions of informants that, as one store owner put it, "We're all the same class of people here; nobody's rich and nobody's very poor." When pressed, however, anyone will agree that there are some individuals who are "better off," "more respectable," or "sorry." That is, while there is general agreement that all people in the valley are equal, nevertheless distinctions of various sorts are made that indicate a ranking of individuals and families.

One of the highest tributes that can be paid a person who has become relatively wealthy is to say that he is "just as common as you and me," and thus compliment his lack of pretension. And the reverse also holds true: one who wears unnecessarily dressy clothing is talked of as "puttin' himself above everybody else," or acting "high and mighty." On several occasions men who had left the Little Laurel to take up permanent residence in Detroit or Cincinnati returned to visit relatives and mentioned the "good life" of high wages and urban luxuries. As soon as they were out of hearing, local men criticized them as having no right "to talk that way about this country here." If one does not offer enthusiastic agreement with the consensual opinion that the Little Laurel is the best place to live, it seems, he is something of a traitor. The only acceptable objection to remaining in the valley is the scarcity of employment opportunities.

Unlike what has been frequently noted for urban social systems—that the major determinant of a person's position is his occupation, that one is in most respects what he does for a living—the Little Laurel presents a pattern of shifting status evaluations and an almost kaleidoscopic image of sifting through many aspects of a person's life to determine where he or she belongs relative to others. It is not occupation alone that determines one's place in the community, but a combination, subject to rapid change, of numerous factors, including family background, knowledge of past behavior, use of leisure time, indebtedness, estimation of honesty and generosity, as well as stability and amount of income.

Steady, well-paying jobs are highly regarded here, but how one spends his money is also important. A father of six children, who earned an excellent income by local standards as a factory worker, was considered "sorry" because he spent much of his leisure time drinking, bought his family new television sets instead of repairing his unpainted and dilapidated house, and allowed his children to go without proper clothing. If one attempts to establish a scale of ranking he finds that informants agree only on the extremes of the scale. Schoolteachers lead the list, followed closely by the most prosperous store owners; at the opposite end are those families who depend for their income on the collection and sale of evergreens, the "galackers." Between these extremes, relative positions, dependent upon the informant, are those whose income is derived from logging, from raising and selling shrubbery, from seasonal work in distant factories, and local entrepreneurs who combine a number of ways of making money. Teachers tend to remain at the top due to the very evident tendency for children of teachers to become teachers. This produces a "dynasty" of teacher families.

Three criteria seem especially significant in establishing the relative rank of any particular person or family: 1. stability of income, 2. amount of income, and 3. moral reputation. It is difficult to see this kind of system as based on class distinctions. Perhaps it is best looked at as a kind of status system, with the various positions in almost constant change. With the exception of those at either extreme, the position of a given individual at any particular time is indeterminate and subject to rapid shifts. If a man decides to give up seasonal migration in order to take a regular job in a nearby textile mill, for example, one can expect change in his prestige. Even if he makes less money than before, it is the stability, the fact that he remains in the valley for the entire year and that his family thus enjoys a greater degree of physical stability, that seems to be important.

This kind of ranking is part of a more general outlook that is characteristic of social relations in the Little Laurel. There is, slicing through every aspect of life, a personalistic view of human relations. Such a view has often been described by anthropologists as obtaining in communities where relationships are carried on face to face, everyone knows everyone whom everyone else knows, and ties between persons are many-stranded or "multiplex." In this, too, change in the Little Laurel is evident. Tourists visit the area every summer, and relationships with them, in stores and in answering their requests for directions and so forth, call for relationships that are single-stranded. It is the obvious discomfort observed among people here when they have to engage in these relations that is striking. It is a mode of interaction they are uncomfortable in, and they say as much about themselves.

Their personalistic orientation is reflected in their attitudes towards occupations. Except for teaching school, which requires preparation through formal education, the concept of one's occupation as a "career" has little significance in the valley. Change in this aspect of life is already underway as some families expect their children to attend college and pursue particular occupations throughout their lives. For the most part, however, the expectation is for one to support himself by engaging in a variety of tasks, either at the same time or serially throughout his life. One holds a job rather than follows a career. Even teachers are not expected to depend upon their employment in the school for their entire income, and all teachers who were heads of families in 1966 were carrying on, at the same time, other activities to gain money. The school principal grew and sold tobacco, the fifth-grade teacher raised cattle for market. Yet it is only here, in teaching, that one can see the concept of career operating, with its assumption of long periods of training, continuation throughout one's lifespan of the same tasks, and the attachment of occupation as part of one's personal identity. For others, an occupation is best described as a job, subject to change as alternate opportunities arise. If a man keeps the same job over many years, or for his entire life, it is due not to conscious training and planning, not to having come to think of himself as having a career. Perhaps it is too much to set teachers apart from this mode of thinking. After all, the principal's father did give up teaching to become a postman, and the apparent reason ("it just got on his nerves") is not at all different from the usual explanation given here for changes of job. And, too, teachers are expected to have multiple sources of income, just as is everybody else. Almost every family fulfills the expectation, although in some cases it is only through selling part of a butchered hog or a few chickens.

When one considers the matter of getting and keeping a job, then, rather different considerations enter than in choosing and training for a career. A Little Laurel man seeking a job wants different information from that contained in an

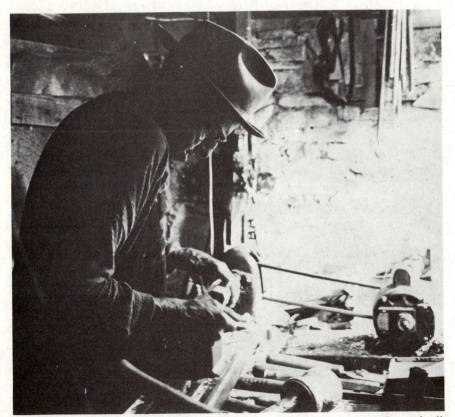

Handicrafts have not entirely disappeared from the valley. This man makes and sells ladder-back chairs. Here he is turning a chair leg on his lathe.

ordinary classified advertisement. The pay is important, certainly, but he desires to learn about his coworkers, he wants personal information about them. As men recount their experiences in Detroit automobile factories or in similar jobs they have held, they almost invariably emphasize the cool, impersonal attitudes of their coworkers and foremen. One man told me that, working as a machine operator stamping out automobile hoods, he had to constantly hold himself back from working as fast as he wanted. "Why, all they wanted was for you to just stay there eight hours a day. I coulda done the work in two hours. Even when there's time off, you can't talk to nobody. They're all different kinds of people." What he lamented was precisely the lack of previous intimate acquaintance with his coworkers. Two young men who were about to leave for factory jobs in the Northeast had, to all appearances, gone about getting the jobs in an urban, matter-of-fact manner. They had applied to the factory representative sent to the area to recruit labor by filling out forms, submitting to a medical examination, and receiving an advance to pay for transportation to the factory. Aside from this procedure, entirely unexceptional to an urban observer, there was a good deal of personal investigation of the work situation. They had learned that they would work under one of two foremen, both from Kent County, and that most of their fellow employees would be men who came from either Kent or adjacent counties. They had investigated the housing situation and located, through a kinsman of one of them, lodging in an area populated by migrants from near the Little Laurel, a few of whom they knew from high school days.

People in the Little Laurel see themselves as distinctive from residents of other sections of the county. In this sense, they can be said to share a "sense of community," an idea of themselves as a category of people different from people

Growing shrubbery for sale is a thriving business in the valley. This field of box-wood, grown from cuttings, is now mature and ready to ship out of the valley.

elsewhere. This is frequently expressed in remarks about the "people up around Chesterville," who are regarded as unjustifiably snobbish and eager to ape urban ways. In the high school attended by children from the valley, boys and girls from the Little Laurel are said to be "backwoodsy" or "rough." During the period of fieldwork, the epithet used for boys from the valley was "the hoods from Little Laurel." A high rate of absenteeism is expected of children from the valley, as it is for other very rural sections of Kent County. For the most part, schoolchildren from the valley do not participate in science fairs, high school literary magazines, and similar urbanized activities. The exceptions are children from families who have moved to the area from outside Southern Appalachia. In sports, however, the valley's students hold high positions, particularly in football and basketball.

A dual kind of change has been at work in the Little Laurel over the past four decades. As local services—schools, politics, post offices—became centralized, what were formerly separate and distinct settlements grew closer together, finally forming a community that includes the entire valley and its ten settlements. The basis for this consolidation, of course, was the development of effective transportation. Without an efficient fleet of school buses, for example, a consolidated school would have been impractical.

In the same period, the links of the valley's residents to the world outside the Little Laurel and Kent County also increased. Migration, both permanent and seasonal, became an accepted alternative to remaining in the valley. Variations in local economic conditions mirrored those of the nation, as people depended more and more upon local factories that were part of giant national corporations. Television and radio have played a large part in bringing to these people information about the urban world outside Appalachia. Communication on the local level, however, as we shall see in the next chapter, has retained many features from an era in which television was unknown.

7 / Communication

A great deal of information is known about the details of people's personal lives in the Little Laurel. Everybody, in the first place, knows almost everyone else. If one sees a strange automobile or person, he can usually accurately assume it is a tourist or other transient. Sometimes, especially with those of different generations, individuals can be identified only with respect to family. For example, a young man came into a grocery store one afternoon, made a few purchases, and after a few minutes the storekeeper asked, "Which one of Roscoe Hensley's boys are you? I know your daddy, but I can't place you."

Many daily activities are highly visible, and hence much information is constantly added to the store of knowledge about people. There is only one main highway in the valley, and it is difficult in many cases to travel from one neighborhood to another without being seen on the highway. Sharp interest is displayed in what transpires along the highway, and for those who live on side roads, in who goes up and down the road. Since what kind of car each person owns is common knowledge, as are his associates, kinsmen, and friends, it is usually a simple matter for anyone within sight to ascertain the comings and goings of large numbers of residents every day. Rather than allow large trees or other obstacles to obstruct a clear view of the road, people often cut away trees and shrubs "so they can see the road," in the words of one old woman, hacking away at a 30-foot locust tree. That this also subtracts from their own privacy by opening it to the casual eye of passersby merits little or no consideration. Houses, too, are almost always built near main roads, and those who construct long driveways to homes shrouded in trees and bushes are thought peculiar. One man used this as the basis of his description of the difference between people of the Southern Appalachians and those living in mountain settlements in the Far West: "Out there, everybody wants to go off and live like a hermit. These people here are friendly, they live right close to each other." To be sure, when houses are near a road in winter, it is easier to drive cars in and out. But this is also a secondary consideration: even those who have to walk to their house across swinging bridges or up steep paths will clip away sufficient forest to obtain a view of the road.

Such easy access to each other's daily activity, combined with the large store of information about the personal background of every individual, provide the basis for the remarkable ease with which residents of the Little Laurel construct highly plausible explanations of each other's behavior. The art of inference is well developed and people are adept at drawing together shreds of information to make a conjectural and circumstantial explanation for whatever occurs. When only two negative votes were cast on a highway improvement bond issue in 1965, the elections officer told a number of his acquaintances that he was certain the two votes came from two young women, both well-known, who "didn't look like they had a idea about the election. They're just bashful about asking, and didn't know what it was they's voting for. Why, they oughta got their daddy to come down with them." At another time, a local bulldozer operator, hired to dig a new garbage pit for a relatively affluent family, made a quick count of discarded beer cans and passed on the news about how heavily the head of household was drinking. During the winter of 1965–1966, Earl Ritchie's black and white pickup truck was observed driving "up the mountain" every morning at about six o'clock with a tarpaulin covering the load in his truck. Two hours later he was seen returning, the load visibly diminished. It was only a few days after his trips began that word was out: Earl was keeping a still on the forested mountainside. The tarpaulin, it was surmised, covered a stack of firewood; the time of travel provided observers with a rough notion of the still's location, and Earl's background was known to include extensive knowledge and practice at distilling "blockade."

Conjectural information of this type goes from family to family through a constant buzz of gossip. The speed of communication, to one unaccustomed to it, is astonishing. When a fifteen-year-old boy shot his brother-in-law in a settlement located at one end of the valley, men in stores at the other end knew of it within fifteen minutes, before the county sheriff had arrived to begin his investigation. The theft of an automobile battery, and an ensuing fight between the thief and the battery's owner, was already being discussed throughout the Little Laurel an hour after it happened.

Financial information, a topic of unusually intense interest, is widely available. To Ed Carter's chagrin, the fact that he paid $30,000 for "that old broke-down Campbell house and 65 acres" was known to any curious resident in 1966. His other landholdings, and the amount of money paid for them, were also discussed in very accurate terms. That he had borrowed from a bank in Tennessee at 7 percent interest, and had thirty years to repay the loan, was part of the general discussion. Almost any adult in the valley can describe the earnings, including amount of pensions, savings, and indebtedness of almost any other resident. Items of this sort are ordinarily not mentioned within hearing of the subject of discussion and, as we shall see in a later chapter, direct inquiries about these and other matters are frowned upon.

Forming a significant portion of the knowledge of each person is his past behavior. Former criminal activity and prison sentences are spoken of in a light vein; there seems to be little imputation of immorality in having "built a year" or two in prison for aggravated assault in a drunken brawl or similar behavior, provided the man involved can legitimately claim to have since become a respectable citizen. Usually incidents of this kind are charged to youthful recklessness. Amusing tales often turn on what a man said to the judge during his trial, or how he was arrested, or how he learned to avoid arrest for the same behavior on subsequent occasions. In the early 1950s two men set up a sawmill in the national forest and began hauling out timber. An automobile inner tube was fastened over the exhaust of the sawmill motor to dampen the noise. Eventually the two were arrested by a forest ranger and brought before a federal judge in Masonville. It was just two weeks before Christmas and one of the culprits pleaded with the judge: "How would you feel, judge, if it was gettin on toward Christmas and you had five young'uns hongry and ragged, with the biggest 'un lookin' like he's gonna eat the little 'uns any minute?" They were released after a stern reprimand and payment of stumpage (about twenty-five cents per tree).

Technological changes have affected the collection and transmission of these bits of information. Automobiles make visitation from one house to another more visible, and increase the speed with which people can pass on what they have learned. The identification of individual cars can, indeed, be said to have increased the ease with which people are identified as they go about their personal business. If one spends a neighborly visit inside the house, his presence is advertised by his automobile parked in the driveway. When men retreat to the forest to drink or gamble, they are more easily spotted than before by the evidence of their cars parked along the roadside.

As the automobile has made secrecy more difficult, so too has the increased use of telephones in the valley. All telephones are on party lines, many of them shared by eight separate households each with its own telephone, and there is no rule of etiquette against "listening in" on whatever conversations occur on one's own party line. As one storekeeper put it, "If you got something to say that you don't want somebody else listening to, then you dang shore ought not say it on the telephone." In addition to party lines, most stores have telephones that are in frequent use by customers. What is said is in effect public, since it must be within hearing of those in the store.

STORES AND STOREKEEPERS

Stores and storekeepers are the primary foci in the day-to-day communication chain that links the entire valley, both within the Little Laurel and with the adjacent areas outside it.

Twelve stores did business in the valley in 1965, ranging from two establishments that are actually small supermarkets to a tiny, dark room where an elderly widow adds a few dollars to her old-age pension. Operating a store is a risky economic enterprise and is depended upon as a single source of income by only two men in the Little Laurel. Other storeowners supplement their income by buying and selling galax and shrubbery, by speculating in land and used cars, and by operating bulldozers. Profits are small for most stores, and failures are frequent. Yet the closing of one store is very likely to be shortly followed by the opening of another, either in the same location (and building) or in a place where none has existed before. Within the year of fieldwork, two of the valley's twelve stores failed and closed, and two new ones opened. A retired storekeeper, who once had the most prosperous business in the Little Laurel, remarked that there were fewer stores now than there had been several decades ago. He explained the popularity of this kind of business as due to the paucity of other opportunities: "When a man set up a little store and it looked like he was making out pretty good, you'd see two or three others open up right around him. It looks like they don't have enough imagination to start something on their own. They just wait till one has something going and then they copy him."

In the larger, supermarket-style stores, one can purchase a wider range of goods than is available in an urban market, including cattle and chicken feed, hardware and tools, motor oil and automobile batteries, children's shoes and clothing, as well as a large variety of groceries, dairy products, and meat. The equipment is modern, and perishable products (for example, bread and milk) are replenished by daily delivery trucks. One of these stores has installed a sandwich bar where one can get hot sandwiches, coffee, and soups. At all but the smallest stores it is usually possible to buy a sandwich made by the proprietor.

Smaller stores ordinarily confine their stock to canned goods, bread, tobacco, and similar staples. When they offer milk and meat, it is from a kitchen refrigerator. These places rely for customers mostly on their kinsmen; tourists and travelers almost always avoid them. Compared to the valley's largest stores, they are dimly lit, and they lack picnic supplies.

Gasoline pumps abound in the valley; six stores are also gasoline stations. Three of these provide, free for their customers, racks where one can change the oil in his car, lubricate, and repair it. Tools can be borrowed from the storekeeper. One is expected, should he use the facilities, to purchase oil from the store.

For the two largest businesses, annual receipts in 1966 were $89,000 and $108,000, of which approximately 8 percent was profit. Smaller stores take in from $3000 to $25,000 per year. The owner of one of the larger stores told of his difficulties in these terms:

> Country stores are caught in a bind these days. We got to keep prices sorta in line with the supermarkets [in Chesterville and other nearby towns], but then we have to give a lot of credit too. Most everybody goes to town at least once a week and they can go to the supermarkets. But we have to tie up a lot of money in credit, and then lose some of it when some of 'em won't pay. Or can't pay.

Credit sales are made by all stores. The largest have, at any given time, from $3000 to $7000 in outstanding accounts. No interest or increase in prices is charged for credit purchases, and some storekeepers even make small loans of cash to their customers from time to time. "You take people around here," explained the owner of a large store. "They don't have much money, but they want the same things everybody else wants, so they have to have it set down [charged]. Why, most of these people can live on fifteen dollars a week."

Almost every storekeeper can cite cases of particular families buying on credit at one store until the owner refuses to extend their account any longer, then moving to another store for another round of credit until the limit is reached, and so on. It is infrequent that storeowners either take legal action or turn over the accounts to a collection agency. Competition for customers is heavy, and impersonal means of collection are regarded as, in some manner, a personal

(Top) One of the numerous stores in the valley with gasoline pumps. Beyond it can be seen the brick building of the only Presbyterian church in the Little Laurel. (Bottom) The proprietor of a much smaller store, located on an unpaved road, that does not sell gasoline and oil.

attack. Not only may the storekeeper lose the business of the recalcitrant debtor, but of a wide circle of his kin, friends, and sympathizers as well. An owner of one store, who depends for most of his income on dealing in galax, told of a competitor who applied legal pressure on his debtors several years ago and reaped a harvest of ill will and loss of business. This has been the usual pattern whenever similar techniques have been tried.

If he has as credit customers those who pull galax, a storekeeper can partially offset his losses by accepting galax in lieu of cash as payment of debts. In some cases, galackers try to circumvent this when they know that most of the money for their galax will be subtracted from their indebtedness. They sell only part of their supply to the dealer-storekeeper with whom they have built up debts, and sell the remainder to another in order to receive cash. "Billy Harris makes a regular thing out of it," said one dealer. "He'll let Dewey [a storekeeper to whom he was deeply in debt] have about half what he's pulled, then sneak off through the woods down here and I'll give him cash for the rest of it." Storekeepers sometimes counter this activity by attaching to themselves, through informal agreements, a number of galackers to whom they advance credit. Since the market for galax is best in the two months before Christmas (when it is bought for decoration), a galacker can sell all he can pull during that period. But the market sags in the spring. Storekeepers can ensure that they receive large amounts of the greenery in November and December by promising to buy certain amounts from pullers in the spring. One storekeeper uses this system so effectively that, when other dealers were paying $1.50 per thousand pieces in November 1966, he was able to keep his rate at $1.40. In return for this temporary loss, he provided each of his regular pullers with a quota for galax in the months of February through April. This is a recent development in the business, for in previous years the price paid to pullers had been fixed by tacit agreement among local dealers. To satisfy the huge and growing demand in 1965 and 1966, however, dealers from outside the Little Laurel made weekly door-to-door efforts to purchase at higher prices than local storekeepers were paying. Not only did local entrepreneurs have to increase their purchase prices, and thus reduce their resale profit, but the quota system was devised to stabilize the locally available supply.

Some dealers—those who have sufficient control over pullers through providing grocery credit or quotas—supply crates and require pullers to pack the galax. Three local dealers make regular weekly calls at collectors' doorsteps to pick up greenery. When this service is offered, the price per thousand galax is reduced by 5 to 7 percent. Once the galax is in a dealer's hands, whether he is a storekeeper or one of the several men who make this their primary occupation, it is resold within a few days to wholesalers and then transported to Atlanta, Cincinnati, Nashville, Baltimore, or points even more distant.

For the small businessman in the Little Laurel, investing large amounts of money in an inventory of greenery is uneconomical, particularly now that profits have been trimmed. In an earlier period, from about 1880 to 1930, profits for local dealers ranged from 20 to 30 percent, but in 1966 they had dropped to 6 or 7 percent. The profit margin is further diminished if one considers the credit extended to pullers and the lack of interest on this investment. In a highly competitive business like storekeeping in the valley, however, where dealing in galax can be seen as an additional means of ensuring customers, precise profit calculations are difficult to make.

STORES AS SOCIAL ARENAS

Far more than churches, with their relatively infrequent meetings, or the school, with its important but occasional ceremonial gatherings, the stores in the valley serve as arenas of social activity. They are locales for daily interaction and communication among large numbers of local residents. Perhaps for lack of alternative sites, local residents rely on stores and their managers for a number of services that are only remotely, if at all, related to the buying and selling of goods. For most residents, stores provide the only easily available telephone service, and customers have been known to "quit trading" with particular stores when the free use of the telephone was refused.

Customers do not enter stores to make their purchases and quickly leave. There is a leisurely air about buying in the valley's stores that, at times, seems to make buying and selling secondary to what appears to be the more important business of visiting. In stores arranged for self-service, local residents often ask the storekeeper for each item, one at a time, and the transaction is carried out during a constant stream of conversation. Customers wander among the shelves, examining new products, pausing to select a soft drink, chatting with others, and frequently take a half hour to complete the purchase of a single item.

The stores are the message centers of the Little Laurel. Information about activities at the churches, the school, or events in the county seat are posted in store windows or remarked upon by the storekeeper. Items for sale, or desires to buy, are mentioned to customers and storekeepers and passed on to prospective buyers and sellers. Lost dogs and strayed cattle are informally "registered" with those encountered in stores, and the information subsequently spreads throughout the valley. Messages for children to come home are left with likely storekeepers to be relayed. Dry-cleaned clothes are deposited by delivery men at stores to be handed on to the owner. Deputy sheriffs seek individuals by first inquiring at the stores. And, passed on through day-to-day encounters in stores up and down the valley, news of fires, thefts, deaths and births, and the comings and goings of the entire population forms the basis for the constant inference and conjecture made by residents about the behavior of their neighbors.

Government functions are also carried out in the stores. Whoever is appointed tax lister schedules visits to most stores before retiring to finish his task with latecomers at his home. The same is true for the registrar, who uses stores as one of his stations for political registration. Balloting on agricultural questions—for example, on tobacco allotment policy—is performed in stores. And, as part of a general educational project of the local poverty program, documentary movies were shown in one store every week for some months in 1966. Poverty workers surmised that the turnout would probably be better in a centrally located store than in the school auditorium.

Nearing his ninetieth year, this storekeeper sells a small variety of canned goods, soft drinks, and staple groceries. Much of his time is spent chatting with customers and reminiscing about the past.

Local men cluster about the stores (except for two which are owned by elderly widows), sitting near a wood- or oil-burning stove in winter, pitching horseshoes or squatting outside in summer. The same men will, in the course of a week, probably participate in such discussion groups at more than one store. Some men —those who pass up and down the highway on logging trucks, for example—spend time in talking to knots of men at various stores. Thus, there are no geographical boundaries to separate these men's groups, although some individuals confine their visits to a store near home or to one from which they buy most goods.

Conversations in these gatherings turn on news of families in the valley, discussions of court cases and arrests in the county, the availability of jobs in and out of the immediate area, and reminiscence about "how things used to be." Land prices are another topic of much interest, especially when the topic is sale of land and houses to "summer people," from whom ever more fantastic prices have become expected.

Women do not participate in this activity, although similar conversations occur when women visit each other at home. In the stores, as in the talk that accompanies drinking and hunting in the forest, men can ignore the religiously based taboos on using obscene language and can discuss topics that are considered "not fit" for the ears of women. One can still discern the influence of the taboos on profanity, however, in the evasive declarations of elderly men who tend to signal emphatic agreement with "*Hell*—oh, yes!" where younger men use "Hell, yes!" To acknowledge the taboos of family life by a swift glance around the store to make sure there are no women (or preachers) present is a common preface to passing on information about sexual behavior or drinking, or to the use of obscenity.

Participation in these men's groups, to which we will return in a later chapter, provides an effective communication network that binds the entire valley. Since most men sit in on several different groups, information is gathered and passed along from one store to another. The storekeepers are key figures in this communication system. By collating bits of news and gossip from their customers, they usually have more knowledge about what happens in the Little Laurel than any one participant in the discussion groups. They can add, from time to time, bits of news to stimulate conversation or to test reactions of the men.

Comparing their present position to what "used to be," storekeepers tend to see themselves as heirs of fallen status. Not only, in their view, was owning a store formerly (until "after the War") much more profitable than at present, but the storekeeper stood near the apex of prestige in the valley. He was the main economic link to the world outside, taking in local produce as settlement of credit accounts and shipping out of the valley a variety of foodstuffs. Stores were buyers of galax and mica sheets, and sellers of almost every good not locally produced. But now, with the press of competition from additional local stores as well as from supermarkets easily reached by automobile, a storekeeper earns less than a schoolteacher and has to supply many services to remain in business.

Yet storekeepers in the Little Laurel, having perhaps lost their previous height of prestige, stand as central points in a highly ramified communications network. They are the prime gossipers of the valley. Gossip includes, in Robert Paine's words,

> 1. talk of personalities *and* their involvement in events of the community, and
> 2. talk that draws out other persons to talk in this way. For a gossiper usually endeavours to receive more than he gives. He has "long ears" and part of his art lies in arranging a constant flow of information to himself. This argument does not deny that a gossiper, still with the intention of receiving more than he gives, often distributes information. In part, he does so in recognition of one of the first principles of information-management. Namely, there is always some information that *he* wishes certain people to possess—e.g., as a reassurance to them about his activities—in order that his, and not their, definition of the situation of the situation prevails. He also distributes information as a move in a series of prestations (Paine 1967:283).

In providing information as a "gift" to those who patronize his store, the proprietor increases his prestige, the accepted estimation of his worth, among his fellows. Acting as a storehouse of knowledge about local people and events, and willing to pass on at least part of what he knows, the storekeeper maintains a constant flow of information to himself. One result is a steady stream of customers, and consequently a barrage of information from a number of sources.

In the fashion of skilled gossipers, however, storekeepers must also know when to restrict knowledge, when to keep a secret. Innocuously, this includes not telling a wife where her husband can be found (if he is drinking or gambling), but promising to pass on a message. Or, when a galacker, known to be a regular customer of another store where his galax would only be converted into credit against his account, wants cash for his galax, to pay him without mentioning what they both know is the reason for the sudden change of store. The knowledge is, as well, kept from the store where the galacker owes money. But the secret-keeping ability of storekeepers often passes these bounds. He can prevent arrests, in many cases, by telling an inquiring law officer that a sought-after man is away from the valley.

Secrets are, for the most part, short-lived in the Little Laurel. The activities of any individual are almost certain to pass into general knowledge sooner or later. What most people aim for, in keeping some knowledge secret, is a short-run advantage. In this the storekeeper is often an ally. When Bradley Edwards wanted to sell his truck, for example, both he and the storekeeper mentioned to no one that Bradley bought, and the truck used, oil excessively. That Elmer Miles retaliated for his neighbor's efforts to sue him in a land dispute case by poisoning the neighbor's dog was kept secret by the two storekeepers who knew of it. Both averred that they thought Elmer's neighbor was in the wrong. When a man has been cuckolded, the matter is frequently known to a storekeeper, who can put together pieces of unrelated information about the couple's whereabouts to make an accurate conjecture of events. Such secrets are usually well kept. If the storekeeper disapproves, he can relay hints of his knowledge, but to bring out the whole story would be to reap disapproval upon himself for "poking his nose in other people's business." Locations of good patches of galax, prices paid for land and livestock, the whereabouts of individuals at various times, and the income of families are all matters about which storekeepers have a great deal of knowledge. They find it to their own advantage not to spread their knowledge too freely.

Indeed the successful operation of a store in the Little Laurel depends very much upon the storekeeper's adeptness in controlling the flow of information among himself and his customers. Privy to many secrets, he can choose what part of them to put into circulation. Receiving information from a number of different sources, he can piece together pictures of events more accurate and detailed than can most other people. By protecting his customers—keeping wives from knowing what husbands are doing or government officials from knowledge of certain illegal activities in the valley—he earns their gratitude and attaches them more firmly to his store. Information about the plans and activities of his competitor businesses is thus, in appreciation for past favors, taken in and used to financial advantage. There are, then, sound if indirect economic reasons for maintaining services—free use of automobile tools, liberal use of the telephone, provision for seating around the stove—that are apparently unprofitable nuisances.

8 / The ethic of neutrality

Where obligations are indefinite and diffuse, as they tend to be in the Little Laurel, refusal to honor them is likely to lead to a correspondingly general breach. Conflict and disagreement, once in the open, are difficult to confine to specific issues or situations. In the past, when most families lived on rather thin economic margins, the necessity for mutual aid meant that a large number of amicable relationships had to be maintained. Conflict, which in most instances might spread rapidly throughout a widely ramified web of kinsmen and neighbors, thus alienating many of them, was detrimental to an individual's economic and emotional security. In open conflict, too, the widely shared knowledge of each other's personal affairs became ready ammunition. The fear of beginning new arguments, and of renewing or perpetuating old ones, seems to underlie the present local custom of trying to avoid controversy or overt disagreement in social interaction.

It is not only among kinsmen that techniques for preventing or ameliorating conflict have developed. Relationships outside the network of relatives are viewed through the lens of kinship; whether with kin, friend, or alien outsider, all social relations tend to be conducted according to a general rule which can be called an "ethic of neutrality." For revealing how this ethic applies to behavior in concrete situations, the conversational topics and styles of expression of local men afford an excellent example. The gatherings of men in local stores, mentioned in the previous chapter, are most frequently encountered, but the same rules apply when groups of men take to the forest to hunt, drink, or play poker, or at the informal political meetings of either party.

A man enters a group with the greeting, "Hello," spoken with a standard, almost stylized intonation, and commonly makes some remark about the weather. If, as sometimes happens, a person in the group is a stranger to the newcomer, no introductions are exchanged. In former years, introductions were unnecessary since the participants had known each other for many years, often from childhood. Much of the conversation concerns news of families in the valley, discussion of county politics, employment opportunities in and out of the immediate area, and reminiscence about "how things used to be." Curious about the identity of a customer in the store, men will sometimes ask the storekeeper, when the unknown person has left, if that was "John Grady's oldest girl, the one that married that boy down in Oaktown," and a detailed discussion of the Grady lineage and the dispersal of his offspring will ensue. With the continuous movement of men from one group to another, information of many kinds is passed up and down the valley.

There is in these sessions an atmosphere of equality that, for the moment, places geographical and kinship solidarity above whatever differences of status might otherwise exist. Men ordinarily call one another by first name or by nickname (for example, Bud, Bullet, Sonny, Spike), and "boys" is the term used to address the group collectively. When taking his leave, a man extends an invitation to the others to accompany him home: "Well boys, come go home with me," or "Let's go cross the river, boys." The response is equally unvarying: "Don't rush off, Bud," or "Stay with us, Will."

Direct questions are seldom asked, except among very close friends, among men who consider themselves "progressive" or "modern," or by very elderly men. Similarly, advice is couched in circumlocution. To gather information, then, one must have a highly developed ability to throw out hints of increasing sharpness. Rather than try to satisfy one's curiosity by inquiring the price an acquaintance has paid for his automobile, a hinting remark is preferable: "I bet a car like that cost a right smart," or "You can't get a car like that for no $200." To provide the correct figure is left to the owner's discretion. In a more common instance, instead of advising a man, "You ought to get a larger wrench for that job," one is less direct: "What a feller needs for a job like that is a heavier wrench." In this way, liability for "telling somebody what to do" is evaded, and no grounds for offense exist.

Great caution is required in introducing subjects of potential controversy. A "prefatory disclaimer" is the customary gambit for opening discussions of this kind and is also a means of relating gossip. "I don't know what there is to hit, but I hear tell that . . ." a person will say, or "Somebody told me such and such. Now is that a fact?" If the reliability of the information is questioned, or if the gossip concerns someone who is kin to a member of the group (who might resent the relaying of derogatory tales), whoever brought up the topic can gracefully disown any responsibility for the information and withdraw into more agreeable matters. Such an introductory style allows one to remain uncommitted to any position until the opinions of others are made known. If disagreement becomes apparent, it can easily be reduced to an acceptable level.

When two close friends sit in groups of this sort, it often occurs that one of the men will "tell one" (an amusing and usually embarrassing story) on the other. The butt of the joke retaliates by remembering an incident which embarrassed his friend. Mock aggression of this sort is a standard feature of close friendship, especially between younger men. To the outsider it appears as a reversal of the ordinary rules of social intercourse, in which the maintenance of tranquility is a paramount goal, and as a mechanism for releasing suppressed hostility toward an approved object. Aggressive behavior between friends—not only verbal battles, but pounding on each other's shoulder or midsection—has a distinctly theatrical air about it, involves the use of elaborate feints and exaggerated movements, and is rarely mistaken for a real attack.

When one inadvertently oversteps the bounds of mock battle, however, he quickly makes amends by turning the insult on himself, meanwhile keeping up the pretense of joking. In a long discussion of county politics one afternoon, to give one example, Carmon Mitchell attempted to make a joke at his friend's expense by saying, "Ollis, why don't you run for jackass of Kent County?" Ollis puffed his pipe silently while the other men roared. Sensing that he had gone too far, Carmon added, "I'll just step down and let you take the office." When a man gains a reputation for responding to such antics with anger, he is labeled a "fractious feller" and either avoided or treated with special care.

Obviously, interaction according to these rules calls for skill in observing subtle, nonverbal cues. Since a person is exceedingly circumspect about stating opinions which might diverge from those of others, a process of "feeling out" the views of each other frequently occupies the men's groups for several hours, or even days, of repetitious hemming and hawing. Ordinarily participants in these groups are well known to each other. That is, their general outlook on a variety of topics can be anticipated and offensive comments avoided. The kinship bonds of those in the group are also known and remarks about specific individuals can be tailored to take account of these ties, including such pertinent information as grudges and long-standing rifts between different persons, illegal activities of those related to members of the group, sexual misbehavior, and the like. When an outsider suddenly enters a group, the response is a period of silence, quite understandable in view of the unplumbed nature of the stranger's kin ties, opinions, occupation, and tolerance for disagreement. Accustomed to taking into account numerous factors before making comments, local men, rather than risk giving offense, prefer to sit quietly or discourse on the universally inoffensive subject of the weather.

The rules of social interaction embodied in the ethic of neutrality can be summarized by listing the restrictions imposed on an individual person:

1. *One must mind his own business.* To indicate that the personal affairs of another are deemed unsatisfactory or displeasing is to threaten insult. Even to ask direct, personal questions is taken as an attempt to interfere in private matters.
2. *One must not be assertive, aggressive, or call attention to himself as separate from the group.* Doing so, a man is open to the charge of "being uppity," "thinking he's better'n everybody else," and of violating the presumption of equality. Not only boasting, which is particularly distasteful, but merely failing to interact frequently is taken as an "uppity" sign.
3. *One must not assume authority over others.* The psychological corollary here is that an individual tends to have a low tolerance for accepting overt demands made upon him. Striving to show no presumption of command, local people are quick to resent any implication of command by others.
4. *One must avoid argument whenever possible, and seek agreement.* Exploration of individual differences of opinion through confrontation and argumentative discussion is an alien tactic. The response to argumentation, as to all offensive attacks, is usually avoidance and withdrawal. When a man has been offended, he has in general two alternatives: to further the dispute by openly showing his irritation, or to keep silent and, in the future, try to avoid contact with the offending person. Physical assault, an escalation of the first option, occurs, as one might expect, most often between youthful men. Perhaps the danger of such combat, both in the likelihood of injury and in the potentiality for divisiveness among kinsmen, lies behind the fact that those most likely to come to blows are also more likely to engage in "roughhousing," and thus make playful what otherwise might be taken very seriously.

Legal action enters on the scene, but rarely as more than a threat. When, for example, a man and his son-in-law get drunk and fight, a wife will call the sheriff for help and perhaps swear a warrant for the arrest of one of the men. A former justice of the peace in the valley says he spent most of his time writing out warrants only to find them lifted within a few days, before indictment and trial. There appears to be no urge to punish an offender through legal process, and the law is used more to threaten and to stop dangerous behavior. Even in cases of persons who persistently write bogus checks or who make a drunken nuisance of themselves in public there is rarely a trial. To pursue these cases to the conclusion of a public trial only compounds the dispute and draws in larger numbers of friends and kin on both sides.

Looking at their interaction from another angle, we can say that the people of the Little Laurel are as yet inexperienced in relating to others in a segmental, partial manner. They bring to every encounter a set of relationships extending through local society; each person's private history, all his sins and shenanigans, are known to almost all those with whom he is in frequent contact. In each situation, due to the relevance of these overlapping bonds, almost the entire life of an individual forms a backdrop to interaction.

ATTACK BY INDIRECTION

The circumspect manner in which hostility is expressed varies from situation to situation, and sometimes reaches an almost Byzantine complexity. When the school principal discovered that the members of one family no longer waved to him as he drove along the valley highway, he immediately concluded that "they're mad at me." He attributed this presumed hostility to his strictness in not allowing the school gymnasium to be used by local adults at night, and this family had been prevented from holding basketball games by his rule. In another instance, a conversation about the evolution of man had gotten to the point of trying to reconcile what a high school student reported from his textbook as 25,000 years since the emergence of *Homo sapiens* with the biblical account. The textbook appeared to most participants to directly contradict the literal truth of the Bible as expressed in Bishop's Usher's chronology (which gives the creation of man as occurring in 4004 B.C.). As evidence for the accuracy of the textbook account, a younger man went home and returned with a copy of *Reader's Digest*, where there appeared an article about evolution. He introduced the magazine with the comment, "Now, I'm not putting this *Reader's Digest* against the Bible, but it is interesting." Throughout the conversation, there was no direct, conclusive statement on the part of anyone; every comment was couched in tentative terms.

For another example of complicated indirection we can look to the case of John Carter's son. This boy, about twelve years old, was punished by the school principal, after several verbal warnings, for fighting on the school grounds. The principal, in his own words, "gave him five licks with my belt. It left a little blue mark on his leg, but he wasn't hurt." The boy's father brought the incident to court where, after a parade of witnesses favorable to the principal, the case was dismissed. There was general agreement in the valley that Carter had brought suit for an entirely different reason. His brother-in-law was janitor of the school, and Carter was envious of his success in handling the job. His legal action against the principal was an attack on the school as embodied in its chief figure. What is important here is not whether or not this was actually the reason for Carter's action, but that it was so generally believed. That is, this kind of indirect action is taken as quite ordinary.

FEUDS AND GRUDGES

Feuding, in the perhaps mythical sense of family pitted against family in repeated physical violence over several generations, is not part of life in the Little Laurel. There is, nevertheless, some indication here that the foundation for long-standing grudges is the same as that for feuding. As Rupert Vance suggests for Southern Appalachia in general,

> The mountaineer lived in a milieu where litigation could not be trusted. Inter-marriage within the confines of their coves left the population connected in a net of kinship groupings. Aggression, insults, and injuries found, because of kinship ties, the community divided into two hostile camps with no neutral buffer group. All who came to act as legal umpire, judge and jury, were regarded as assuming the mask of impartiality in order to protect a kinsman or wreak vengeance on an enemy. There remained the resort to feud, and judges, thought to be partisans, were sometimes shot down on the bench (Vance 1932:250).

The rule of "good sportsmanship," involving fighting to a conclusion and then continuing a relationship as if nothing had happened, finds little support in the Little Laurel. Games and sports among schoolchildren, too, are played with ferocious partisanship, with the will to win dominant over the desire to uphold the rules of the game. Any match between school teams is likely to be peppered, during the game and for weeks afterward, with charges of cheating, and umpires and referees are frequently accused of favoring the opposing team.

Forgiving and forgetting are not characteristic of old disputes; grudges, with the associated lack of interaction of those concerned, remain from generation to generation in some cases, and riddle any particular neighborhood with crossfires of petty spitefulness and hatred. Vengeful attacks are customarily secret: a man might awake to find his dog shot or poisoned; a storekeeper will see some of his customers quietly disappear after he has used legal action to collect debts; a wooded area suddenly flames in the night, fired by a grudge-holder.

The history of a twenty-year series of disputes between two men, both storekeepers in 1966, can serve to illustrate the pattern of hostility. On election night in 1946, a group of recently returned Army veterans had gathered in one of the small schoolhouses to watch the counting of votes. Ross Randolph, one of the veterans, remembers that they were hoping for the victory of one of their number who had campaigned for county sheriff. The man with whom he was later to be bitter enemies, Luther Bennett, was a special sheriff's deputy, on duty in the school to keep order. As each vote for their friend was announced, the veterans would give off loud encouraging comments ("another one for our boy"). As the noise continued, Bennett's father, a Republican like his son, told Ross that they would have to quiet down. Ross, a Democrat like most of the assembled veterans, replied with a crude insult, and was rebuked by Luther. Shortly a general melee ensued, Luther's holstered pistol was taken from him, and Luther and Ross squared off for a fist fight. The elder Bennett, however, had gotten the pistol and thumped Ross with it on the back of his head. Ross whirled and slapped the old man, sending him sprawled into a corner. The fight soon involved most of the men present and went on for a half hour. Since that time, Ross and Luther have engaged in a series of fist fights, court cases, and finally, economic competition.

Sometime during the early 1950s, according to Ross, "I got religion and went to Luther to call it quits, but he said he never would forget it. He's one of the dirtiest, meanest sons-of-bitches there is around here. He carries a gun right now, and you never know if he's crazy enough to use it or not." After one of their many renewals of open conflict, a fist fight in which both were drunk, Luther charged that Ross had hit him with a large stone (a common legal allegation here). The case went to court, with a number of witnesses testifying for each side, and was finally decided in Ross's favor. In 1965, after a local gasoline "price war," the prices at the valley's gas pumps again resumed their normal range, except for the prices at Luther's store, where gasoline remained cheaper. Ross was convinced that the "unfair competition" was part of the undying hostility borne him by Luther. The two men, however, rarely confront each other, and the grudge is fueled for the most part by scandalous remarks each makes to his associates about the other.

GRUDGES IN POLITICS

When one holds political office, he is subject to the same restraints and judged by the same standards of conduct applied to all adults. It is assumed, and generally correctly so, that an elected official will give preference to his kinsmen and friends in filling appointive positions. A corollary of this view is that there is, to varying degrees, a tendency to make no distinction between the incumbent of an office and the office itself. Thus, those who hold political office appear to have a personal stake, almost a kind of ownership, in their position. But, as a check on this attitude, there also exists a widely held notion that any political office should not be occupied too long by the same person. This idea appears to be based on a broader conception of mankind as inherently evil and inevitably drawn into evil behavior (due to "original sin"). The temptations of political office, of the possibility of personal enrichment from the public purse, are well-known and regarded as too strong for most men to resist for long periods of time.

One is always ready, it seems, to impute base motives to those with whom he has had a falling out, and politics is simply the most easily observed arena where these charges and countercharges are made. The political primary campaign of the Democrats in 1966 was such an occasion, a time of stress when past misbehavior was recalled and used to discredit the claims of one's opponents. Two Democratic factions emerged in the Little Laurel during the campaign and only after months of battle were they able to join forces in the general election against the Republicans. The factional struggle was nonetheless so intense and damaging that the Republicans swept the county offices for the first time in twelve years.

A significant part of the campaign process was to dredge up ancient sins committed by the opposition and parade them in conversation before the voters. This is, to some extent, a common political maneuver; mudslinging is an old theme in American politics. Yet in this valley it had a distinctly personal air, and was carried on by both factions without letup for several months. Wherever men gathered, one among them was likely to mention the time Nate Renfroe "raped" Josie Smith (an allegation only; there was no prosecution); when, in a previous term of office as sheriff, Joe McIntosh had been charged with misappropriation of county funds; when Wallace Rayford had broken into a summer cabin and "built six months on the road gang"; or when James Mathis had burned the contents of two ballot boxes to promote a favorable election outcome. Such past offenses, in the course of daily life, appear to be largely forgotten; one hears of them only in the heat of political campaigns.

The Democratic faction in office faced a challenging coalition of Democrats who declared themselves in favor of "reforming our school system." Supporters of each faction spoke of themselves as motivated by the highest ideals of citizenship. Each saw the opposition as consumed with a disreputable desire for personal gain. The challengers planned to elect a new school board that would hire teachers on a basis of merit, rather than for reasons of kinship or political reward. They were castigated by the faction in power as trying to reinstate school administrators and teachers who were their own close kinsmen and who, in a previous period of employment, had embezzled the schools of large sums of money. There was some merit to the arguments of both sides, and the challengers represent a useful example of the expression of personal ill will in contexts that seem irrelevant.

The "reform" faction's leadership consisted of ten men, each with an old grudge against one or more of the leaders of the opposing faction. Their reform goals were belied in conversation after conversation by their plans, after they won the election, to discharge those teachers most obviously engaged in political battle. (The teachers, of necessity, lined up—some openly, most covertly—with the faction in power.) By the same token, the reform leaders were joined together, in eight of the ten cases, by multiple bonds of kinship and friendship, and had been involved over a span of many years in a number of joint activities. They were all members of the Masonic Lodge in a nearby town; four of them hunted bear together every winter. Several of these men were close kinsmen of leaders of the opposing faction (one man in fact was a brother of the opposition's chief), but there was general knowledge that a breach existed between the kinsmen in each case. Political antagonism for these men was simply another facet of a pervasive and often bitter enmity between them and their estranged relatives.

ELECTION GAMBITS

As one expects the worst of one's opponents, so he takes steps to counter their plans. The reform faction in 1966, in a secret meeting a few days before the Democrats held their township meeting (to choose delegates to the county convention), drew up elaborate plans to ensure the election of reform delegates. They would submit a list of nominees to the meeting, then quickly move for nominations to cease before the opposition could propose their own list. When one man demurred, saying he thought this tactic unfair, he was told that "that's the way they'll [the opposition] do it if they have a chance." Only the possibility that "they'll get so mad at us they'll turn Republican" convinced the men not to carry out this plan. Throughout the secret meeting, however, the tone was one of setting traps to foil whatever plans the opposition might have. It was agreed, for example, that they would attempt to have votes cast by standing, rather than written, ballot. This would, as one man pointed out, "make the women stand up together—they wouldn't want to sit there when somebody right next to them is standing up." This technique would also provide a public display of support and opposition to the reform faction.

At the township meeting, the reform faction carried the day. With open balloting by standing, there was ample opportunity to cajole and threaten people to vote "properly." Two reform leaders, both of whom were galax dealers with a number of poor families economically dependent on them, surveyed the assembly at every vote, tugging sleeves of their clients and whispering threats ("maybe you'd better get up") when necessary to arouse the voters. Similar moves were made by the opposition. Each ballot was counted by a representative from the two factions, and the count differed with each ballot, with each representative increasing his own side's votes and decreasing those of the other. Only when the vote was counted by a minister was it accepted without question. As a conciliatory move, after having all their delegates chosen, the reform faction offered a motion to pledge the delegates to stand for reintroduction of the primary system in the county and to discard the existing county convention method of choosing party candidates. (For state and national offices, candidates are not chosen by the convention system, but each party, Republican and Democratic, holds primary elections.)

When Democrats and Republicans clash in elections, there are many activities on polling day that are questionable at best, and sometimes simply illegal. Charges and countercharges of fraud and corruption in the way elections are conducted pour from both sides. The township registrar, for example, is repeatedly accused of retaining on the list of eligible voters some people who have been long dead and of engaging in illegal procedures in obtaining absentee ballots from those who have moved away from the Little Laurel. Just before election day, the registrar does make several trips to towns in various parts of the state, collecting absentee ballots from former voters of the valley. Contrary to election laws, which specify that when a voter needs assistance in casting a ballot his relatives should take priority in providing the help, officials of both parties eagerly offer and give aid to the elderly and enfeebled. Ballot boxes are sometimes carried out of the school, where polling takes place, to cars in order to allow ill voters to place their ballots in the box.

But the most constant accusation heard on both sides concerns the outright purchase of votes. Recollections about past instances of success and failure in vote-buying, humorous anecdotes of how one or the other side was outwitted in vote-buying efforts, and quotations of the variation in prices of votes are endemic. The registrar, recounting one past incident, said

> I was out canvassing and run up on this feller off in a holler. He said a Republican had been there and give him a brand new dollar bill if he'd just stay home on election day. So I told him maybe he oughta come in and vote, and keep the dollar anyhow. And he did. Voted Democrat, like I figured he would, too.

On another occasion, a Democratic party leader recalls that he was at the polls on election day and saw a man, known as a stalwart Republican, sidle up to another man approaching the polls, reach into his pocket, and hand over some money. "I could see as well as anything that he just bought a Republican vote. So I met the feller as he come up to get his ballot, and told him if he would just vote the opposite of what he'd been told, I'd give him another dollar and then he'd have two."

In the election of 1966, several men in both parties had volunteered to "drive on election day," that is, to provide transportation to the polls for constituents who might not otherwise vote. When the Democratic drivers gathered outside the school that morning, a party official met them with instructions and money. Handing each man ten dollars ("for what gas you use"), he gave this suggestion: "Now, boys, getting some of these people in to vote is just like catching a bird— you've got to put a little salt on their tails. If any of you need more money, just come see me." Although nothing was directly mentioned about buying votes, the implication was clear. Votes were purchased during the day for payments that included, to various individuals, six boxes of snuff, a load of firewood, and the promise of an interest-free loan of twenty-five dollars. Cash payments ranged from two dollars (for the vote of an impoverished widow) to ten dollars (for a household that contained three eligible and willing voters). Offers to buy voters are invariably put indirectly, commonly phrased as "making it worth your while" or as offers of neighborly help (in the case of such items as firewood).

An abundant supply of liquor and beer also aided both parties in their quest for votes. At about midday, a car pulled up to the school, parked, and the trunk was opened to reveal a full load of intoxicants. Cans of beer were sold for fifty cents, and undecided voters were treated to one or two beers before they were guided to the polls. The county sheriff, a Democrat up for reelection, visited the township polls twice during the day, but he and his deputies studiously avoided noticing the portable tavern. Beer was purchased by both Republicans and Democrats, and both sides had ample supplies of whiskey in a number of cars and trucks.

MODERN ORGANIZATIONS IN THE VALLEY

Gradually knitting themselves into the general social and cultural patterns of urban America, local people still do not move easily in the kind of formal, voluntary organizations created for specific and limited ends that are so widespread a phenomenon in the United States. The premises of voluntary organizations, in conducting business by the formal steps of parliamentary procedure, are contrary to those of traditional groups in the Little Laurel, and the organization of "community action groups" or other formal organizations intended to carry out programs of general community benefit is an unrewarding task. Such groups stir little interest and their life is brief.

An effort was made in 1967 to form a Little Laurel "community club," sponsored by the county agricultural agent as part of a state-wide program of public improvement, but no local persons could be coaxed into accepting the chief offices. A Methodist minister, who presided over the initial meeting of the few people willing to participate, reluctantly took over the president's position "temporarily." The office of secretary-treasurer was pressed on a retired New York woman who has lived in the valley for ten years. Both these persons were classified as "outsiders," and were thus able to take on the role of club officer without risking offending anyone. Committee chairmen in every case were named under duress, after repeated demurrers from those nominated; for several committees the problem of authority was solved by electing several cochairmen. All officials were elected by acclamation.

The organizational vitality of strenuous discussion, dependence upon a core of reliable workers who direct routine operations, and the ready acceptance of delegated responsibilities by a larger number of members, some of the characteristics of successful voluntary organizations, are alien ways of achieving group goals for people in the Little Laurel. The appropriate behavior in such organizations—the minimal individual assertiveness, tolerance for the divisiveness induced by majority-minority decision-making techniques—is contradictory to the ethic of neutrality. Even in the well-established framework of politics, concessions are constantly made in adapting to local patterns of interaction.

The recent case of community organization repeated the failures of similar efforts in the past: attendance at the community club's meetings dwindled from the original twenty-four to fifteen at the second meeting, then to five. No arguments appeared to mar the peace of the meetings, and interest in the organization, never enthusiastic or widespread, soon disappeared.

The utilization of "outsiders" to solve problems of the assumption of authority in the Little Laurel is quite similar to the organization of voluntary groups in Pentrediwaith, Wales, Ronald Frankenberg's *Village on the Border* (1957) where "strangers" and "outsiders" (a distinction made less clearly in the Little Laurel) are useful as scapegoats. When groups fail to reach their goals and dissolve, the strangers are assigned the blame and those who are deeply involved in the reticulate obligations of the village can escape any hint of "trying to boss another." In this way, the villagers' view of themselves as harmoniously unified is maintained.

In the Little Laurel, the category of outsider includes the small proportion of the population who have retired in the valley, like the New York woman mentioned above as secretary-treasurer, as well as the "summer people," who occupy for a few months each year a total of about forty-five cabins in the valley. But rarely do these people participate in local organizations. Most keep to themselves, remaining essentially uninvolved in local social life.

TACITURNITY AND LACK OF EMOTION

Particularly in contexts of musical performance, the stark absence of emotional expression by Southern Appalachian people has been widely noted. Ballads of deep melancholia are sung with a straightforward lack of emotional expression that often astounds listeners, even while they judge it more effective as a communicative device.

Yet it is not only in these rather specialized situations that the "taciturnity" of mountain people receives comment. It is frequently encountered in descriptions of the personal attributes of these people. One student of Appalachia ascribes it to time spent by themselves:

> The taciturnity of mountain people has so often been remarked upon that it hardly seems worth dwelling on. However, the relation of isolation, which mountain life brings, to this lack of expression, may be a matter of great interest. The mountain man who works by himself in the field or forest all day, or the mountain woman who goes about her household duties without adult companionship might easily fall into the habit of little speech (Weatherford 1955:63).

If the Little Laurel is not entirely atypical, however, quite the contrary seems to be the case: mountain people spend a great deal of time with others, usually with people they have known for most of their lives. More to the point, Cratis Williams, in a discussion of the Southern Appalachian regard for "observing manners and exchanging civilities," suggests a relationship between taciturnity and nonverbal communication:

> Extremely modest about their achievements and embarassed by praise, they want to be urged to display their abilities, and they are so sensitive to criticism that even a lifted eyebrow will cause them to recoil suddenly to taciturnity with intensely wounded pride (Williams 1962:19).

Given the restraints placed on interaction, as embodied in what is called here the ethic of neutrality, the reluctance of people in this region to express their emotions as openly as do urban Americans is quite understandable. Nonverbal communication is especially important in the Little Laurel, and the residents are adept at apprehending and interpreting nonverbal clues. In these circumstances, it is to one's advantage to exercise severe control over the sending of messages, just as he is extremely sensitive in receiving them from others. Taciturnity, too, makes a good deal of sense, if one's audience is alert to insult and offense, intended or not.

It is not at all that people in the Little Laurel lack emotional response, or that the forbidding gloom of the mountains has sealed their lips. For very sensible reasons, however, they are careful in what they say and do. Depending on subtlety and nuance rather than merely upon content, in both speech and behavior, they might be said to be more acutely attuned to their social surroundings than many other Americans.

9 / Beyond the valley

Since the streams of migrating whites from Pennsylvania and the eastern coast first spread into the Little Laurel in the late eighteenth century, the valley has continued to maintain contact with the outside world. Although to a large extent self-sufficient in the production of the bare necessities of life, people here have never been fully so. Even when the westward march of settlement bypassed them in the nineteenth century they remained dependent upon outside markets for their products. Changes in market conditions brought rapid response in the valley; when a product no longer commanded good prices, energy was shifted to the production of another. Ginseng was succeeded by galax; mica slipped out of favor and was replaced by the excavation of feldspar.

Their language, too, has not been as unchanged through time as is usually supposed. Tales of the preservation of "Elizabethan English" in the Southern Appalachians are simply romantic fabrications. There are a number of words and expressions still in use in the Little Laurel and adjacent settlements that are probably retentions from an American English which was far more widespread in the nineteenth century and earlier. Such words as "blackguard," "cuckold," and "high sheriff" are frequently heard in the valley and bespeak an earlier era when they were widely known and used. Other words are perhaps more restricted in their former usage. "Daresome" for dangerous, "unthoughted" for unintended are rarely heard, even in the Little Laurel, but their meaning is never in doubt. One scholar suggests that the speech of Southern Appalachia can aptly be seen as part of a cultural tradition that is generally conservative:

Folk wisdom, words familiar on one level to Americans generally but which have distinctly local meanings in the highlands, epigrams, pungent phrases, wholesale conversion of nouns to verbs, are generally archaic survivals from colonial times which may be found in the vernacular speech recorded in Restoration drama and early American fiction as well as dialect dictionaries. Like the diction and rhythmic intonation, the content of mountain speech is a survival of what was once general rather than something that has sprung up in the mountain country. Not peculiar to the mountains, it, too, differs only quantitatively from the content of the speech of semiliterate folk descended from the same stock but living in other isolated areas of the United States (Williams 1961:13).

MARKETS AND JOBS OUTSIDE THE VALLEY

The availability of markets for local products has been a major influence in dictating what will be produced in the valley. For some decades in the nineteenth century, ginseng was pulled from the forests, dried, and shipped to distant markets. Wholesale collecting with little thought of replacement led to a decline in the availability of "sang," and efforts to gather it declined as other products grew in importance. A number of distilled plant saps were sent from the valley to urban markets, both in the Southeast and in the cities of the Northeast. When it became evident that, with far less energy and time, the same money could be made by pulling and packing such small plants as galax, local producers quickly responded. Galacking soon became an important occupation, although only a part-time one for most people, in the Little Laurel. Technology killed the markets for some products—tan bark is one example—and interest shifted to others. When prices for chestnut lumber skyrocketed, it was sufficient to lead a few Little Laurel men back into the forests to drag out and sell half-rotted logs.

As with forest products, market fluctuations outside the valley effectively determined what would be dug from the ground. Mica gained in importance, but the introduction of the mineral from cheaper sources in India led to a rapid decline in prices, and consequently to less mica coming from the slopes of the valley. As an important material in the construction of bombsights and other implements of war, mica again assumed significance when the federal government established a stockpiling policy during World War II and the Korean War. After sufficient quantities of mica had been stockpiled, however, the guaranteed price was discarded and mica mining quickly declined in the Little Laurel. Feldspar mining, too, has been phased out in response to changes in technology and markets. Only when a chemical flotation process made its production economically profitable did mining companies invest the capital necessary to strip feldspar from the hillsides near the valley. Even today, it is unimportant as an occupation for people in the Little Laurel.

Remote from urban centers as it appears to be, the valley is still strongly affected by strikes and other economic events in industrial America. When the airlines suffered a large-scale strike in early 1966 there was an immediate drop in the local production of galax. Storage of the plant requires large buildings with equipment for maintaining even temperatures, and these soon filled. Among galax dealers and pullers alike, no topic of conversation was more important during this period than the possibilities of a settlement of the strike. Similarly, the availability of employment in distant cities becomes known quickly in the valley. Just after World War II the favorite city for those seeking well-paid jobs was Detroit. But since that time there has been a shift to other cities, and Chicago, Denver, and Cincinnati have each received large numbers of migrants from Southern Appalachia. In 1966 the Far West—primarily Washington and Oregon—was considered the best territory to look for employment by men in the valley. About twelve families had established a pattern of seasonal migration, spending winter months with kinsmen in the Little Laurel and moving with their families to Oregon and Washington for the spring and summer.

Improvements in transportation have brought economic opportunities into the valley itself. Tourists flock to the Little Laurel in greater numbers every year, and land prices continue to rise as more land is sold to outsiders for the construction of summer cabins. With credit purchases of trucks relatively easy, local entrepreneurs seize opportunities throughout the Southeast for selling shrubbery grown in the valley. As with galacking, large numbers of people depend upon shrubbery growing for part of their income, but only those who buy and truck it to distant points outside the valley make this full-time employment. In 1966 several men began making weekly trips in their pickup trucks to farm markets in Alabama and Georgia, buying quantities of tomatoes, watermelons, and peaches and reselling them to storekeepers in the Little Laurel. And, just as dependent on modern transportation, one man in the valley makes a regular winter trip to Florida, where he peddles stones he has collected in the valley to eager buyers. In this way he manages to finance an annual two-month vacation in Florida.

ATTITUDES TOWARD OUTSIDERS

Aside from their rather ambiguous feelings of resentment and welcome toward those who settle in their midst for summer vacations, people in the valley share a general attitude of remoteness from business and government organizations. The federal government, for example, is always known as "they." Less frequently, the same attitude can be discerned about the state government. "They won't let the governor of this state have more'n one term," is a typical phrasing of this attitude. It is as if these people have little involvement in the selection and operation of national or state government bodies. In spite of the presence among them of agents of the government, particularly as forest rangers and employees of the National Park Service—which hires a number of local people during the tourist season—they consider the government itself as quite distant from themselves. Consequently, there is little compunction to be truthful with, for example, federal government investigators who try to determine how forest fires were set, or military policemen searching for draft dodgers and deserters.

But this attitude is perhaps more forcefully expressed in stories told, with hilarious admiration, of how local residents have bilked large corporations. A middle-aged widow contracted with a large corporation to build herself a "shell house," a small frame building without interior partitions or finish. As security, she mortgaged a small tract of her land to the construction company. As an informant related the story,

Well, Lucille had her a place all bullnosed off level, where she wanted them fellows to build her little house. When they brought the lumber, they put it down the hill from the level place. Then, about two days after that, the carpenters come and built the house where the lumber was. Well, let me tell you, they never did get Lucille to pay for that house. She got it free, because they didn't put it where she wanted it. Of course, they took that other piece—the one she put in the contract. But she got herself a house free and clear.

The tendency among people in Southern Appalachia to be, as one commentator puts it, "careless enough in handling the truth," (Weatherford 1955:67) has received special attention. In a report written after a summer in one poverty-stricken section of Kent County, a college student remarked that "boys [aged twelve to seventeen] without exception would frequently lie to me and deceive me. Most of the time it was hard to detect the deception and to separate fact from fiction in the stories I heard. . . . The concept of honesty was meaningless to them, it seemed. This problem was especially troublesome when I tried to find out touchy facts about certain people." Once accustomed to the extraordinary reliance people here have upon nonverbal communication, their resentment of direct requests for information, and the intimate knowledge of one another's activities they share, these remarks take on sharper focus. What outsiders label a habit of "lying" is better understood as another part of the tendency of mountain people, including those in the Little Laurel Valley, to think of themselves as distinct from those who come from other regions. They have indeed been encouraged, through long years of commentary on their quaintness and old-fashioned mannerisms by visitors from urban America, to regard themselves as different, and so feel no need to open up to outsiders.

SKIRMISHES IN THE WAR ON POVERTY

In the 1960s the plight of people in the Southern Appalachia came to national attention. Efforts of the federal government to eliminate hunger and want, and to raise the general standard of living in the mountains—heralded by articles and headlines in newspapers and magazines—brought troops of "community organizers" to the "hills and hollers" of Appalachia. A few decades earlier, missionary efforts of church groups had, in order to raise funds to ameliorate conditions of poverty in the mountains, advertised the mountain people as ignorant and impoverished. News notices again portrayed, in photograph and story, the mountain people as universally destitute and helpless. And, once more, the picture thus painted was resented by prosperous and poor alike. Knowledgeable people in the Little Laurel resent the tendency of such organizations to broadcast pictures of the worst houses, the most ragged and sickly children, and the most pitiable households as representative of the entire region.

The poverty program in the Little Laurel was undertaken by a regional organization, composed of paid and volunteer workers over an area of four counties. Under a well-paid director, this association assigned VISTA (Volunteers in Service to America) workers to various sections of the area, wrote progress reports, and applied for financial grants from the Office of Economic Opportunity in Washington. In a mimeographed report issued in 1967, the directors of the organization admitted that its personnel had "spent two frustrating years of attempting, with small success, to create the group spirit, the feeling of self-confidence and self-importance, the hope and aspiration that individuals must have before concerted community effort for improvement is possible." Disappointment was their reward.

Part of the difficulty in bringing about rapid change in Southern Appalachia is due to certain characteristics of many of the poverty workers themselves. The "community organizers," who are in most frequent contact with the poor families of the region, are generally young and politically liberal or radical. Many of them are former or peripheral members of New Left organizations; they speak with indignation about the urban middle-class attitudes which they seek to escape. The visible effects of the increasing involvement of Appalachian people in the industrial economy of urban America, and the concomitant acceptance of the luxury products of that economy, are somehow distasteful to these youthful idealists. After all, their very presence in Appalachia is often a sign of their personal rejection of the values of the urban middle class, and they regard the mountain people's closer and closer approach to those values with dismay.

Workers in the antipoverty program have based their efforts on preconceived images of people in Southern Appalachia. Lacking familiarity with the intense dependence upon kinship bonds, they tend to see a lack of organization. Church groups are relatively ineffective in drawing large numbers of people into social activities or even Sunday services. Politics is prey to notions of almost "private ownership" of political office. Few agencies exist which can act as neutral mediators in disputes and arguments, and once begun conflict is likely to spread quickly and remain as a divisive element for many years. Perhaps most importantly, the antipoverty workers have failed to grasp the distinctive styles of communication that operate in Southern Appalachia.

One skirmish in the war on poverty by the four-county agency can serve to point up the radical differences in communication styles between antipoverty workers and mountain people. When application was made to the Office of Economic Opportunity for a large grant to set up a "poor people's newspaper," objections from Appalachian newspaper editors and political leaders were overpowering in their horrified accusations that such a newspaper, being financed by government funds, would automatically become a voice of official propaganda. Rhetorical allusions to freedom of the press, replete with quotations from Thomas Jefferson, belched across the region's editorial pages for days after the proposal was announced. A lawyer in Kent County lamented, in a letter to the editor of the Masonville daily newspaper, that

> When the United States Government goes into the field of broadcasting and the publication of newspapers we can kiss freedom and democracy goodbye. It would only be the first step to the establishment of an iron-clad dictatorship.
> Every honest man and woman in this county, regardless of whether Republican or Democrat, should lose no time contacting our members of Congress and letting them know how we we feel about this scheme of swiping our money for the purpose of debauching our country.

What had been proposed was something much more analogous to a corporation or labor union paper—a tool with which to organize the poor and strengthen their self-confidence and consciousness of themselves as having common problems. The newssheet was to have been written and produced by people with low incomes and distributed free to over 3000 low-income families in the four counties. With the immediate and sustained outcry from influential leaders, soon resulting in an objection voiced on the floor of the United States Senate, the proposal was withdrawn before it could be acted upon by the OEO.

If, however, one takes into consideration the prevailing styles of communication among the people of this area, particularly the poor, a far more cogent argument against the project could be made on the grounds that it would have been an ineffective means for organization. Southern Appalachian people, if we can generalize from the Little Laurel, rely on oral communication. They receive little information on a regular basis from printed sources. This is emphatically the case with those in the lower income categories, but applies as well to families which are relatively affluent. The proposal for a poor people's newspaper was ill-conceived because personnel in the poverty program lacked detailed knowledge of the interactional and communicational styles of those they wanted to aid.

This kind of misunderstanding, of course, is not limited to such highly publicized incidents as the foiled newspaper. It is a constant and continuing problem, and can be easily seen in the analysis on which the plan for a newspaper was based. The proposal decried the "historic and continuing physical, social and psychological isolation not only from the world at large, but from each other," said to characterize local people, and considered the passive behavior of small church congregations as the "only significant tradition of group participation" in the area. This ignored entirely the existence of a wide range of occupational, recreational and cooperative groups, developed through kinship bonds, which form the social matrix for Southern Appalachian life.

Since the basic organizational principle for these various groups is kinship, there is a strong tendency for urban-reared antipoverty workers to overlook its importance in mountain communities. The rights and obligations of kinsmen to each other are often seen as a burden by highly mobile urbanites. But if one lives out his life among a large number of kin, depending upon them for a great variety of economic, political, and emotional services, kinship is quite reasonably the most significant relationship one can have with other people.

By assuming that traditions of cooperation and collective organization are absent, the community organizers sought to impose on mountain people an urban form of association. This seemed to them an appropriate and necessary first step. Yet the recipients of this attention found it difficult to understand; many of them see as self-evident the problems to be solved to bring about increased affluence. They know very well that rapid change is already underway.

When people in the Little Laurel are asked what they consider the major problems confronting them, the main barriers to economic success, they invariably point to the need for improvements in the local schools, primarily in the direction of making them more like urban schools, and in the local highway system. Better highways are required, as one man in the valley said, "so's people can get to their jobs easier. It won't be long before almost every family's got people working away in the plants."

As for the schools, they tend to see a direct relationship between education and employment opportunities; an increase in number of years of schooling is expected to result in a corresponding increase in future income. The schools, they say, should be improved as a means of making the next generation wealthier. Many of these people have felt, in their own occupational experience, the need for additional education; job promotions are closed to those who lack elementary skills in reading and arithmetic.

In spite of the unanimity among Little Laurel people about what problems exist, community organizers seem to them to suggest solutions which are inappropriate and unrelated. Being for the most part young and idealistic, the organizers are intent on instituting "participatory democracy" in this part of Appalachia. The solution of specific, concrete problems can wait until proper organization is established. Resort to the use of existing groups for the identification of common problems and the organization of collective effort to solve them is almost never tried.

One exception which I observed to this general statement should be described. An intelligent and perceptive young man found in 1966 that his efforts to organize Stony Branch, the poorest settlement in the valley, were repeatedly unsuccessful. Although he had prior assurance that an OEO grant to repave the local road would be forthcoming, he was unable to induce the neighborhood to elect officers for a "community improvement organization." Only after agreeing that whoever volunteered for the office of president could resign immediately after the road was finished was he able to complete the OEO's requirements for the grant application. The man who finally submitted to the office of president, an industrial worker with some experience in urbanized groups outside the valley, would assume no more authority than to allow his name to be used on the application. But cases like this, in which the reluctance of local people to assume authority over their neighbors is taken into account, are rare.

While people in the Little Laurel, as in all of Southern Appalachia, are eager to adopt the products of urban society—the labor-saving gadgets, the trinkets of amusement, and the higher income of industrial employment—they balk at taking on the social reorganization entailed in modernization. They resist the attempt to replace the bonds of kinship and long-term friendship with the impersonal but efficient relationships demanded by modern industrial society. Despite their steadily growing involvement in industry, they insist upon judging men on highly personal and moralistic grounds.

Numerous examples of a refusal to take on the routine activity and rigid structuring of time required by employment in a factory are available in the valley. A man with several years' experience on Detroit assembly lines returned to the valley to open a small store, thereby reducing his income by more than half. In commenting on assembly line work, he said: "I never had a job where it took so long to build eight hours." In another case, a father of six children worked in a textile mill for two months before quitting. "I just couldn't stand to have nobody tell me to get there every day at the same time, and have 'em hollerin' at me all day," he confessed. He decided to cut and sell firewood instead. Although his income suffered a sharp drop, he gave no indication after ten months of self-employment that he would return to an industrial job. As his own boss, he feels he controls his life far more than was possible in the mill.

It is this kind of thing the poverty workers find difficult to understand. In their view, the man—and others like him in similar circumstances—was trading relative affluence for an uncertainty of income and employment that appeared irresponsible. Yet, in extensive discussions with them, I have heard the poverty workers express admiration for men like this who refuse the routine work of the sort deemed characteristic of middle-class America. They view the mountain people's enthusiastic acceptance of urban products—television, canned and "instant" foods, gaudy cosmetics, new cars—sadly. Wanting to eliminate economic hardship, they are nevertheless unwilling to lead the people of Appalachia toward urban life styles.

Perhaps there exist alternatives for this situation, in which the Little Laurel, and all of Appalachia, need not become simply another copy of industrialized, rationally organized urban America. If so, it appears that far more basic changes in the national economy and political structure will be required to realize them. Change in the Little Laurel Valley, meanwhile, proceeds at a quickening pace and the outlines of urban America become clearer, but the agencies of change in large part are industrial employment, improved highways, and television, not the poverty program.

References cited

Ball, Richard A., 1971, "The Southern Appalachian Folk Subculture as a Tension-Reducing Way of Life," in *Change in Rural Appalachia: Implications for Action Programs*, John D. Photiadis and Harry K. Schwarzweller, eds., pp. 69–79. Philadelphia: University of Pennsylvania Press.

Davis, Allison, R. B. Gardner, and M. R. Gardner, 1965, *Deep South: A Social Anthropological Study of Caste and Class*. Abridged edition. Chicago: University of Chicago Press.

Frankenberg, Ronald, 1957, *Village on the Border*. London: Cohen and West.

Gluckman, Max, 1956, *Custom and Conflict in Africa*. Reprint. New York: Barnes and Noble, 1967.

Kephart, Horace, 1922, *Our Southern Highlanders*. 2d ed. New York: Macmillan.

Kernodle, R. Wayne, 1960, "The Last of the Rugged Individualists." *Harper's Magazine*, October.

Lanman, Charles, 1856, *Adventures in the Wilds of the United States and British American Provinces*. Vol. II. Philadelphia: John W. Moore.

Olmsted, Frederick L. 1860, *Journey in the Back Country*. New York: Mason Brothers.

Paine, Robert, 1967, "What is Gossip About? An Alternative Hypothesis." *Man* (New Series), 2:278–285.

Toynbee, Arnold J., 1946, *A Study of History*. Abridged edition. New York: Oxford University Press.

Vance, Rupert, 1932, *Human Geography of the South: A Study in Regional Resources and Human Adequacy*. Chapel Hill: University of North Carolina Press.

Weatherford, W. D., 1955, *Pioneers of Destiny: The Romance of the Appalachian People*. Birmingham, Alabama: Vulcan Press, Inc.

Williams, Cratis D., 1961, "The Content of Mountain Speech." Part IV of Mountain Speech. *Mountain Life and Work*. Vol. 37, No. 4, Winter.

———, 1962, "Mountaineers Mind Their Manners." Part VI of Mountain Speech, *Mountain Life and Work*, Vol. 38, No. 2, Summer.

Recommended reading

Caudill, Harry M., 1963, *Night Comes to the Cumberlands: A Biography of a Depressed Area.* Boston: Little, Brown.
   The author, a lawyer and political maverick of eastern Kentucky, makes an impassioned plea for ecological conservation of the Cumberland Plateau in Kentucky, a center of coal mining. Excellent survey of the historical background of coal mining, written in colorful prose.
Fetterman, John, 1967, *Stinking Creek.* New York: Dutton.
   Useful mostly for the fine photographs, this is an anecdotal book by a photographer-journalist. Contains interesting details of daily life in a small and impoverished settlement in eastern Kentucky.
Kephart, Horace, 1922, *Our Southern Highlanders.* 2d ed. New York: Macmillan.
   First published in 1913, this remains as a key source for firsthand information on Southern Appalachian life for the early part of this century. Living for a time in western North Carolina and eastern Tennessee (the Smoky Mountain region), Kephart presents a sympathetic and entertaining portrait of the people.
Pearsall, Marion, 1959, *Little Smoky Ridge: The Natural History of a Southern Appalachian Neighborhood.* University, Alabama: University of Alabama Press.
   In many ways, this is one of the best books on the Southern Appalachian people. Based on fieldwork carried out by an anthropologist in 1949–50, it concentrates on relationships among family and kinspeople. The author has become one of the experts on the region and on developmental anthropology.
Photiadis, John D. and Harry K. Schwarzweller (eds.), 1971, *Change in Rural Appalachia: Implications for Action Programs.* Philadelphia: University of Pensylvania Press.
   A collection of articles dealing with change and the prospects for the future of Southern Appalachia. Parts I and II concern institutions in Appalachia and the relationship of the region to other parts of the United States.
Schwarzweller, Harry K., James S. Brown, and J. J. Mangalam, 1971, *Mountain Families in Transition: A Case Study of Appalachian Migration.* University Park: Pennsylvania State University Press. Building on Brown's earlier study of a small community in eastern Kentucky, this book traces the effects of migration of people from this community to urban areas of Ohio and the results on their home neighborhood. Because of its lengthy time perspective, a valuable work.
Stephenson, John B., 1968, *Shiloh: A Mountain Community.* Lexington: University of Kentucky Press.
   A sociological study of change in a western North Carolina mountain settlement. Reared near the Appalachian region, the author is sympathetic and knowledgeable about the people he describes, and has based his work on several

months of participant-observation. His work is especially insightful on the mixture of "traditional" and "modern" life styles, although his typology of family life seems a bit strained.

Weller, Jack E., 1965, *Yesterday's People: Life in Contemporary Appalachia.* Lexington: University of Kentucky Press.

A result of many years of missionary work in the Southern Appalachians, this is a well-written account of interactional styles in, for the most part, West Virginia. Unfortunately, the author tends to apply generalizations on this part of Appalachia to the entire region.